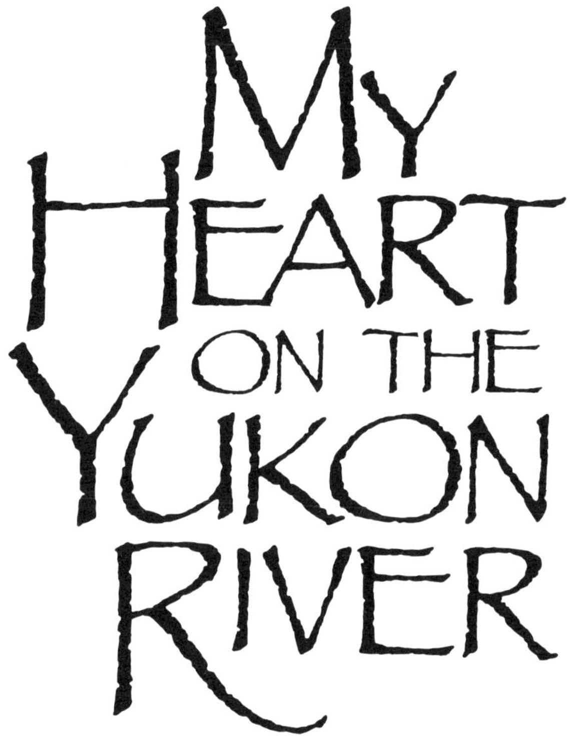

My Heart on the Yukon River

Portraits from Alaska and the Yukon

Monique Dykstra

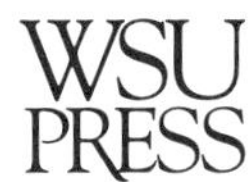

Washington State University Press
Pullman, Washington

Washington State University Press, PO Box 645910, Pullman, WA 99164-5910
Phone 800-354-7360; FAX 509-335-8568

First printing 1997

Printed and bound in the United States of America on pH neutral, acid-free paper.

Library of Congress Cataloging-in-Publication Data

Dykstra, Monique, 1964-
My heart on the Yukon River / by Monique Dykstra.
p. cm.
ISBN 0-87422-157-9 (pbk. : alk. paper)
1. Yukon River (Yukon and Alaska)—Pictorial works. 2. Yukon River Valley (Yukon and Alaska)—Pictorial works. 3. Yukon River Valley (Yukon and Alaska)—Biography. 4. Yukon River Valley (Yukon and Alaska)—Social conditions. I. Title.
F912.Y9D95 1997
971.9'1—dc21

97-26116
CIP

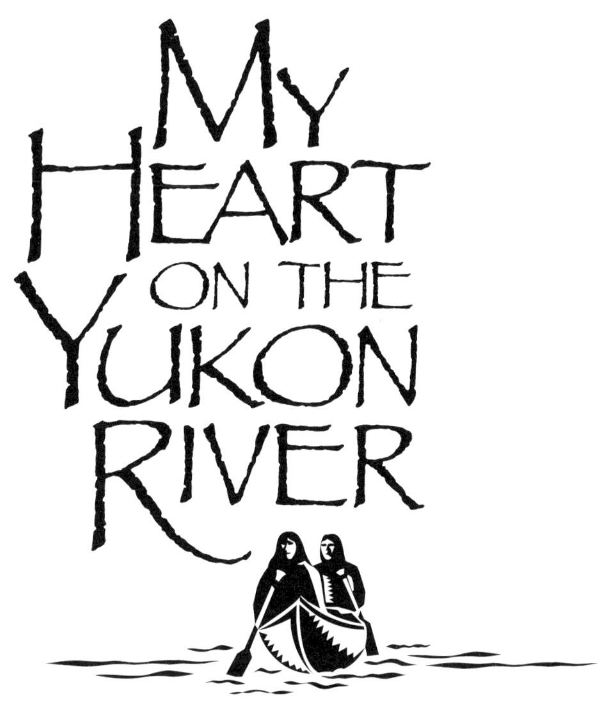
My
Heart
on the
Yukon
River

To my parents:
Peter and Gail

Table of Contents

Acknowledgments

I am deeply grateful to the following persons and organizations, to whom I wish to express my thanks:

To the people of the Yukon River for your gracious and overwhelming hospitality. Without questioning or judging, you welcomed us into your lives, fed us full to bursting, obligingly answered our questions, and stood patiently while I made portrait after portrait. It is my sincerest hope that you like the book.

To the Canada Council for funding my project. It never could have happened without your support. To Richard Holden: thanks so much for your encouragement.

To Kodak Canada, NDG Photo, and Trek-Hall Photo for donating film to the project.

To Patagonia, Mountain Equipment Co-op, and 3 Vets Sporting Goods Store for donating outdoor gear.

To Kanoe People for a generous discount on the canoe.

To Hageland Air for free flights in Alaska.

To Kathleen Usher: thank you for your help with the interviews.

To the staff at WSU Press: thank you for being so delightful to work with. To Mr. Lindeman: particularly you, Glen!

To Gabriel Tordjman for an unwavering interest in the book, your faith in me, and for teaching me how to separate the "blubber from the meat." You are a fine editor and a wonderful friend.

To Arden Ford for sage advice, publishing knowledge, and, most of all, gentle kindness.

And, to the following for their editorial input, help, and encouragement: Mike Carroll at Raincoast Books, Jim Reil, Gillian Robinson, Michelle Gagnon, Suzanne McAdam, Martin Segal, David Robinson, Libby Oughton, Brian McNeil, Don Corman, Donna Miller, the staff at Dawson College, and Trooper Tom.

Introduction

"Yeah, I'm still in the Yukon, but now I've got a dog team and a trapline. Why don't you come up and visit?"

"I . . . I don't know," I said, wedging the phone between my shoulder and ear while lacing my boots. I was late for my waitressing job at the Town Pump, a busy nightclub in Vancouver, British Columbia. It had been six months since David and I had broken up after dating sporadically for eight years.

"I've really got to go, David. Let me think about it. I'll call you back as soon as I can, okay?"

David was still in my mind as I ran through Gastown's misty, cobblestone streets. When I reached the Town Pump and swung the heavy front door open, I was slammed by a wall of noise: Dead on Arrival, a raucous punk band, was playing that night. From experience I knew I would make no tips and would spend the night fighting my way through a sea of black leather and a rainbow's selection of colored hair.

Halfway through my shift, a band member started a chain saw and began chopping things up on-stage. As I pushed my way through the crowd with a full tray of drinks, someone's fist punched towards the ceiling in a rocker salute, hitting my tray squarely.

Even before I finished cleaning up the broken glass, I knew I was going to the Yukon.

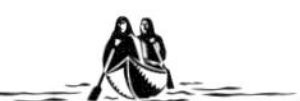

The street lamps made a procession of perfect cones down Dawson's deserted main street when the bus dropped me off in front of Arctic Drugs on an icy December night in 1986. After piling my bags into the drugstore's doorway, I went in search of David.

My boots sounded like gunshots on the wooden boardwalk as I passed a multicolored row of shops, many with towering false fronts from the gold rush days. Nothing moved except the swirl of snow that spun and twisted in the streetlights. Then a sudden tide of amber light spilled into the street as two men, loudly cursing the cold, left the Downtown Lounge. That was where David was waiting for me. I saw his hair first: rust colored, it was longer than normal and it stood straight out from his head like a brush.

My boots left traces of snow on the crimson carpet as I passed windows hung with red velvet drapes and walls decorated with gold embossed wallpaper and turn-of-the-century paintings. David was using dramatic hand gestures to describe something to the bullet headed man sitting across from him when he saw me.

"Monique," he said, his hands suddenly dropping to the table.

"Hello David."

"How are you?" he asked, tilting his head and looking at me warily.

"I'm okay. How are you?" Maybe this visit was a mistake. Hadn't we broken up?

"Couldn't be better," he growled. "Want a drink?"

Half an hour later, David tucked his stiff, woolen pant legs into his boots, pulled a succession of ragged sweaters over his head, then struggled into an army surplus parka.

"The dogs are tied up behind the bus station," he said, forcing his hair under a toque. "Wait 'till you see them!" The initial awkwardness of our reunion was fading quickly.

Eight huskies slept curled in the snow, noses under tails. Harnessed to the long narrow toboggan, they stood up and shook off the snow clinging to their fur as David loaded my bags.

"Okay, hop in!" he said, tucking an old sleeping bag over me. I grinned into the darkness, feeling like an Eskimo princess. Then David yelled, "LEEEEEEETSS GO!!" and the dogs took off.

We slid around the corner of the building, shot across the main street, took a quick right, and galloped along the riverbank. Except for a small beam shining from David's headlamp, it was pitch dark. All I could hear was the sled creaking over the hard packed snow and the dogs' toenails scraping against the ice. "HAW, PORKY, HAW! LETS GO, PORKY! HAW! HAW!" Suddenly, the sled veered sharply to the left and shot into mid-air, depositing Porky and the other dogs, David, the sled, and me in a tangle at the bottom of the riverbank. Such was my reacquaintance with David and my introduction to the Yukon River.

I had lived in the north before, but it wasn't a place I would have returned to had it not been for David. In the winter of 1985 I had hitchhiked through the huge and empty landscape of the Yukon and Northwest Territories.

Eventually I settled for a few months in the far north at Inuvik, Northwest Territories, where I shared a small house with another woman. I had a job at a fast food restaurant, while she worked at the supermarket.

On our days off we often went dancing at the bars. Though I had never seen people drink so much, I soon accepted it as normal. One day my friend stopped me in the frozen food section of the supermarket. Tears rolled down her cheeks when she told me she was raped at knife point by one of the local boys. We both left Inuvik and the north soon after.

But Dawson seemed different. A small community of 2,000 residents, "Dawson" is a historic town on the banks of the Yukon River. The river valley is lush with life—fish, birds, and game abound. Inuvik, on the tundra, seemed barren and lifeless by comparison. Many people I had met in Inuvik seemed desperate and sad and would drink themselves senseless to escape themselves and the town. I saw little of that hopelessness in Dawson. Here I met people who seemed fully alive and in control of their destinies, especially the people who made their homes in the bush. They appeared strong, independent, and resourceful.

After my visit with David had stretched to over two months, I flew to Vancouver, packed up my apartment, and returned to the Yukon in April. I was totally unprepared for the explosion of my first northern spring. David and I moved from a trailer into "Cheta's" charming, abandoned tree house. Although still piercingly cold at nights, the ice soon left a nearby creek and filled the tree house with a soothing murmur. Cool green light streamed through the screened windows as swollen buds burst into leaves and new patches of wildflowers sprung up daily beside the path I took to town to look for work.

One warm spring morning I stopped at a coffee shop after applying for a fire fighting job with the Yukon forest service. Swirling cream into the steaming black liquid, I wondered how good my chances were at getting a job there. While I didn't have any direct experience, I'd been a tree planter in British Columbia for several years and had spent two summers leading canoe trips in northern Ontario. My thoughts were interrupted when a dark haired boy poked his head into the restaurant and yelled, "The ice is going out!" Food, talk, and coffee cups were abandoned as everyone ran down to the riverbank.

Shelves of ice soared down the river like great ships, shrieking and grinding as they collided. As they rammed into the bank, the ground shuddered beneath my feet.

"Wouldja look at that one!" bellowed the old guy next to me, waving a beer bottle towards a particularly large, gray chunk. "Oh, it's good to see break-up, isn't it?" he said after taking a long swig.

I wholeheartedly agreed. It was the first of many times I would be awestruck by the immense power of the river.

A few weeks later, the forest service sent me to a fire-fighting training course outside Whitehorse. Under fragrant pine trees, we were taught everything from fire suppression theory to wilderness first aid. One instructor, Terry Hanlon, taught us hand tool use and maintenance. Besides Terry, I met many other remarkable people at the training course. Kristen was one of them. I saw her again at the post office in Dawson a few days after the training ended.

"Hey, Kristen, how's it going? You ready to start work on Monday?" I asked.

"I'm not going," she said, grinning. "I'm going to solo kayak to the Bering Sea instead!" Not long after, as I watched her kayak disappear downriver, I knew someday I would have to follow her.

Over the next four summers I fought more than 100 fires for Forestry. None was more memorable than a 1,100 hectare fire near the Fortymile River in August 1991.

"How do you feel about taking the fire at Fortymile as a training exercise?" my boss asked, peering at me through narrowed eyes and tugging at the end of his immaculate beard.

"Uh, sure! It'd be great!" I answered with what I hoped were equal measures of confidence and enthusiasm while inside I was filled with sudden, sharp terror.

After breakfast the next day, 65 fire fighters, 3 helicopter pilots, and an excitable French Canadian cook all looked to me expectantly. While most faces were encouraging, hostility radiated from a few. Many of the fire fighters had far more experience than I. As well, none had ever been on a fire with a female Fire Boss. Yukon Forestry had hired only a handful of women in the many years since its inception. None I knew of had ever run a campaign fire.

I divided the fire into four sections and assigned a crew to each. Although trees were still burning near a mining camp in the northwest section, most of the work consisted of patrolling the perimeter for burning roots or "smokes." Mop-up, as this part of fire fighting is called, is the least interesting part of the job.

Like the crew, I felt apathetic and bored after ten days of patrolling the fire from the helicopter. Not a single "smoke" had been reported all day. Resting my elbows on my knees, I cupped my chin in my hands and fought to stay awake. As I was drifting off to sleep, I saw something flicker in the distance. Forcing my eyes open, I saw a curl of smoke in the northwest quadrant.

"Hey! Jim Cathers, do you copy?" I yelled into the headset microphone. "Where are you Jim?" Why wasn't the northwest crew boss responding?

"I'm having lunch at helipad two. What's up?" he finally answered.

"There's a big smoke in your section, Jim. We're coming to get you."

When we touched down on the helipad, Jim ran towards us in a half crouch, carrying a chain saw in one hand and a half-eaten sandwich in the other. His crew followed him, and a few minutes later we were flying over the smoke.

"It doesn't look good," Jim said to me over the crackling headset.

What an understatement, I thought.

"Yeah, if it gets to that stand of spruce, it could burn for miles along the top of that ridge," I replied in a flat, calm voice that didn't seem like my own.

We circled the smoke, looking for a place to land, but there was none. "Okay, Jim. You and the crew will have to walk in from the pad. We'll bucket water on it until you get here."

After dropping Jim and the crew off at the helipad, we flew back to see the curl of smoke had grown into a column. From inside the helicopter, I could hear the WHOOSSHHH sound the trees made when the flames raced up the branches and shot out their tops. Sparks rained on the surrounding trees, and they too began to torch. We had to start bucketing, and fast.

The pilot landed on the bank of the Fortymile river and clipped a 300-gallon collapsible bucket beneath the helicopter. He flew over the river a few minutes later, then slowly lowered the bucket into the water. As soon as it was full, he headed for the smoke and dropped a sheet of water on a flaming tree. It was like trying to put a campfire out with a teaspoon. All we could do was attempt to hold the fire until Jim and his crew arrived. Frantically, we flew back and forth from the river until the pilot spotted a flash of blue below. It was Jim.

"Cathers portable, Dykstra portable," I said into the headset microphone.

One of the tiny figures below put down a chain saw. "Go ahead. This is Jim."

"Yeah, how's it looking down there, Jim?"

"Oh, we should be able to get it in a couple of hours," he answered. As I relaxed into my seat again, I remembered an old crew boss's words: "No napping on the fire line!"

On my days off I often canoed down the Yukon River. The current is strong near Dawson. Even without paddling, it's possible to cover 30 to 40 miles in a day. Once, I got as far as Eagle, Alaska—100 miles away. I daydreamed of paddling to the sea and of spending months instead of days floating down the river as Kristen had done.

"The river is magic," she wrote that summer. "I can't explain it. I wish you could see it."

She ended up falling in love with a fisherman 1,000 miles downriver and never did get to the Bering Sea, although one day she says she will.

David and I spent the winter on a trapline after my first summer of fire fighting. A local trapper and fisherman, Tim Gerbeding, gave David permission to trap in one of the valleys on his vast trapline and to stay in an abandoned cabin nearby. It was three days' travel from town by dog team.

In the early 1970s, Tim and a school bus of friends had left Colorado for Alaska in search of a self-sufficient life for themselves in the northern wilderness. After unsuccessfully scouring Alaska for the perfect location to build their new community, they came to the Yukon. They found their version of paradise in the Coal Creek valley, 50 miles down the Yukon River from Dawson.

Except Tim and two others (named James and Mike), everyone left after the first winter. Unperturbed, the three men began building their cabins. Tim chose to build on the valley floor, close to the Yukon River. Mike picked a hilltop a mile up Coal Creek from Tim's place, and James found a good building site in a neighboring valley. Mike lasted one more winter before moving to Fairbanks, Alaska. Tim and James are still in the Yukon. No longer actively trapping the area, they still spend the summers at Coal Creek, running one of the most successful salmon fisheries along the Yukon River.

Armed with Tim's vague directions, we went to look for Mike's cabin on a frigid December morning.

"If we can't find it, where are we going to stay for the winter?" I asked, after tramping through the snow for several hours.

"I don't know," David answered, stopping to catch his breath. "Tim said it was about a mile up Coal Creek. I just don't get it."

When we finally found the cabin, we discovered why it had taken so long: Mike had built his home into a hill, which made it almost impossible to see except from straight on. We had walked by it several times without noticing it.

David lit a kerosene lantern after stepping over a deep snowdrift inside the cabin. The flickering light revealed a

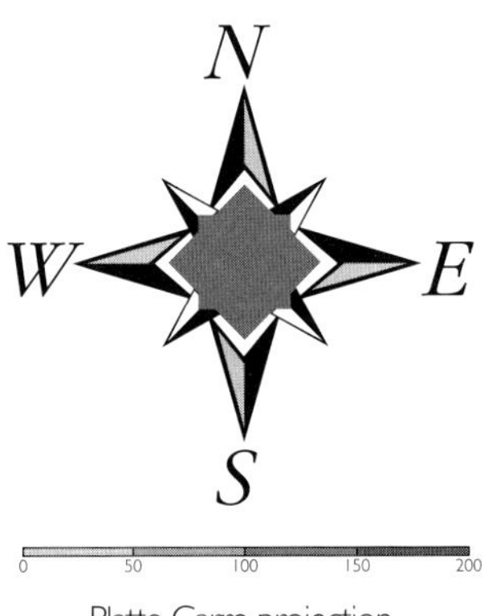

Platte Carre projection

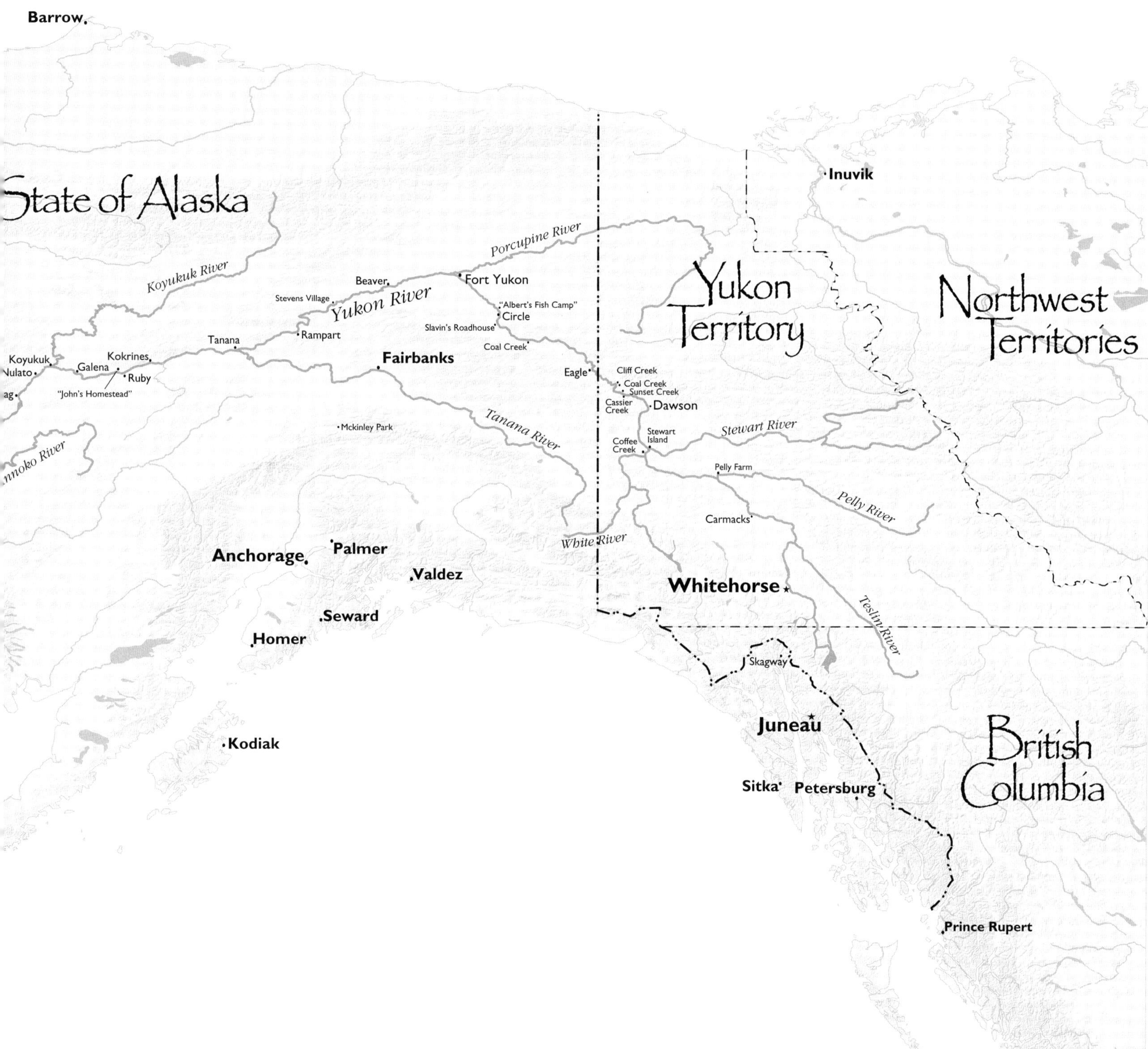
Barrow
State of Alaska
Yukon Territory
Northwest Territories
British Columbia
Inuvik
Porcupine River
Koyukuk River
Yukon River
Beaver
Fort Yukon
Stevens Village
"Albert's Fish Camp"
Circle
Slavin's Roadhouse
Rampart
Coal Creek
Tanana
Fairbanks
Koyukuk
Nulato
Kokrines
Galena
Ruby
"John's Homestead"
Eagle
Cliff Creek
Coal Creek
Sunset Creek
Cassier Creek
Dawson
Stewart Island
Stewart River
Coffee Creek
Tanana River
Mckinley Park
Pelly Farm
Pelly River
Carmacks
White River
Anchorage
Palmer
Valdez
Whitehorse
Teslin River
Seward
Homer
Skagway
Juneau
Kodiak
Sitka
Petersburg
Prince Rupert

table, some chairs, a wood stove, and a bed built high off the ground. As my eyes adjusted to the gloom, I glimpsed a carpet of mushrooms on every surface. My heart sank. While I wasn't expecting a palace, I thought it would be nicer than this.

"It's a little rustic, eh?" said David ruefully. It looked a little better when we cleaned it up.

Once our gear was unpacked and we had settled in, we went to explore the trapline. After a few days in the yard, the dogs were ecstatic to be out on a clear, sunny December morning. The toboggan cut a deep swath through the sparkling snow as we slid between the thickly wooded banks of Coal Creek. Overhead, the cloudless sky was a pale, delicate blue. David's singing clashed dramatically with the beauty of the day: *"I met my girrrrrrll by the factory walllllll . . . dreamed a dreeeeeamm by the old canaaaaaaal . . . dirty old towwwwwwnn . . . dirty old towwwwwwnn."*

We planned to stay in a cabin at McGuinness Creek that night. By nightfall, when we still hadn't found it, we decided to make camp.

The spruce trees spread deep shadows in the bright moonlight as we made camp in the shadow of a large, round hill. David went to get firewood while I got the dogs ready for the night. By the time I was finished, David had placed caribou skins beside the huge fire he built and was making supper.

"Eat it before it freezes," he said, handing me a hot bowl of soup.

After gulping the soup down, I looked around for the tent.

"We're just going to sleep out here like this?" I asked, noticing he'd laid out our sleeping bags on the caribou skins.

"Don't worry. I'll keep you warm."

"You'd better," I said, "it's at least 25 below!"

I whipped off my parka, balled it into a pillow, then dove into the sleeping bag. As soon as I warmed up, I popped my hands and head out, fished my contact lenses out of my eyes, then looked up at the blurry stars. After wiping a light mist of snow from my face, I immediately fell asleep.

In the middle of the night, the sound of howling wolves woke me with a start.

"David!" I said, shaking his shoulder, "Wake up!"

He mumbled something and buried himself deeper into the sleeping bag. When the howls began again his body stiffened. "What was that?"

"Wolves! I think they're up on the hill!"

"Jesus!" he whispered, fear in his voice. "The dogs! I've heard of wolves sneaking into camp and killing entire teams!"

The wolves never did come into our camp, but they did keep us awake as they howled throughout that memorable night. Over the course of the following week, we found the cabin at McGuinness Creek, set some traps, and explored the upper part of Coal Creek. Then, when our food ran low, we decided to return to Mike's cabin.

A frozen marten lay in one of the traps when we checked it on our way back. While David was ebullient, the sight of the animal's graceless death saddened me. The marten had been caught by one delicate leg and its tiny mouth was frozen open in a wide, soundless snarl. In places, the animal's prized fur was soiled by its own blood and urine.

"She's frozen right to the trap," said David, tossing the animal, trap and all, into the toboggan.

Later, when the small creature thawed, David showed me how to skin it. With a small knife he made a cut near the marten's anus. Then, after disengaging the tail, he peeled the fur away from the animal's body in a single piece. Like rolling down a stocking, I thought.

Although trapping wasn't for me, I didn't feel it was wrong for others to do it. Trapping is a harsh, demanding life with little financial reward. People trap for a variety of reasons: because it's what they've always done, for the love of the hunt, or simply because they love being in the wilderness. Yukon trappers most frequently catch marten, but also trap for the elusive wolf, wolverine, and lynx.

It didn't surprise me that trapping fascinated David. He had been drawn to old fashioned and traditionally male occupations before. As soon as he was old enough, he left Toronto for New Brunswick to learn the arcane craft of wooden boat building. When his one year apprenticeship was finished, David moved to Dawson where he began hunting, fishing, and trapping. His first full trapping season was the winter we spent on Tim's trapline. David was completely happy. Life in the Yukon wilderness was a challenge and an adventure which satisfied his romantic nature. There, like no place else, he was in total control of his life. He could do or be whatever he wanted.

The winter at Coal Creek was difficult for me. Although I recognized the purity of living self sufficiently and delighted at being in a beautiful and remote place, I began to feel, as the winter progressed, that I was tagging along after David rather than sharing his dream. For years, I'd been wanting to go to school in Montreal to study photography. When we came out of the bush the following spring, I asked David if he'd move to the city with me. When he said no, I went alone. David stayed in the north.

From 1990 to 1992, I attended the Dawson Institute of Photography in Montreal. I studied during the winters and returned to my fire fighting job in the summers. Although I missed David, I felt I was doing the right thing. Photography was fascinating. Good portraits seemed able to capture a tiny piece of a person and imprison it on film. I finished school in the spring of '92 and won the award for best graduating portfolio of the year.

David's sister, Elizabeth, lived in Montreal. One night in December 1991 she invited me over for supper. The wind rattled the kitchen window while I sat slicing tomatoes for a salad. Pushing the lace curtain aside, I saw fat snowflakes falling under the streetlights and thought wistfully about the Yukon.

We ate a dinner of lasagna, salad, and dark bread at Elizabeth's big wooden table, washing everything down with cold German beer. Later, as we sipped coffee and ate small pieces of bittersweet chocolate, she asked, "What would you like to do most in the world?"

"I'd like to canoe down the Yukon River," I answered without hesitation.

"So do it! Make it a photo project and try to get a grant from the Canada Council!"

I stared at her. "I'd love to do portraits and interviews of people living along the river," I said, my excitement building. "Do you really think they would give me the money?"

In answer, she turned on the overhead light, got a pad of paper, and pushed the dishes to the far corner of the table. Then, sitting with her pen poised over the page, she said, "Can't hurt to ask."

Whitehorse to Carmacks, Yukon Territory

"My Heart" Milepost 0, Whitehorse • *Christening "My Heart"*

"What kind of photographs do you want to take?" Kathleen asks, squeezing the tea bag against the side of her cup.

"Portraits," I reply, pushing a plate of oatmeal cookies to her. A cold March morning in 1993, we are sitting in my purple and yellow kitchen ("It's very—um—er, *Mediterranean,"* my roommate pronounced while we were painting it).

"Just about every photographer who goes to the north shoots big, glossy color landscapes. I want to make a book of portraits, and they've got to be in black and white," I say, warming to a favorite topic. "Color is too gaudy to show what's really inside a person and—"

"And you want me to help with the interviews?" Kathleen gently finishes.

"Exactly! We'll call it a job. While I can't cover your travel or personal expenses, I can pay you slave wages of $500 for the summer. What do you think?"

Kathleen's mass of brown curls bobs in agreement long before I get to the end of the sentence. "How can I refuse an offer like that?" she says, grinning and raising her cup. We clink tea cups to cement our partnership.

"Kathleen's perfect," I say to my roommate, Sue, as I stack the cups and plates into the dish rack. "She's really friendly, she's got some canoeing experience—she's even done some interviewing before." For several summers, Kathleen worked as a naturalist at St. Lawrence Islands National Park in Ontario. One summer she helped put together a history for a Park publication on one of the largest islands by interviewing its long-time residents.

"I'm sure she'll be great," Sue agrees, spreading a thick layer of cheese on some Pumpernickel bread. "Now, about the phone bill . . . "

Knowing the high cost of food in the north, I decide to buy all the supplies in Montreal, then ship everything to the Yukon. We put the food into six boxes and ask David Robinson in Dawson to ship the boxes to us along the river as we need them. Breakfast will be oatmeal and coffee, and lunch will be pan bread, trail mix, and leftovers. For dinners, Kathleen prepackages meals such as pasta with sausages and rice with beef jerky.

A little nervous about possible water damage, I divide the film equally between the six food boxes. Kodak has donated 100 rolls of film to the project and NDG Photo in Montreal gives me a generous discount on 200 additional rolls. I package the film in doubled Zip-Loc bags, place the bags inside waterproof plastic food containers, then stuff the containers into canoe bags.

My camera gear includes a Hasselblad with an 80mm lens, a Mamiya C33, a Nikon with a telephoto zoom, a Seconic light meter, Metz and Vivitar flashes (accompanied by a case of batteries), two diffusion umbrellas, light stands and tripod. I pack the camera gear in a waterproof, impact resistant case, then put the case into a waterproof canoe pack. The umbrellas, light stands, and tripod go in another canoe bag. My friend and teacher at Dawson College, Martin Segal, generously offers to be my disaster insurance—should anything go wrong with my camera gear on the river, he'll ship me whatever I need by the quickest means possible.

The interviews will be recorded on audiocassettes, then transcribed later. One hundred 90-minute tapes are spread equally between the six food boxes. In the canoe, Kathleen stores the tape recorder, tapes, notebooks, pens, and model release forms in yet another waterproof bag.

Patagonia donates two gorgeous sailing slickers to the project and Mountain Equipment Co-op gives me a $100 gift certificate. Over 25 canoe manufacturers are petitioned for a free canoe. While I get plenty of encouragement, I don't get a boat. In the end, a Whitehorse rental company, The Kanoe People, sells me a canoe for a reasonable price.

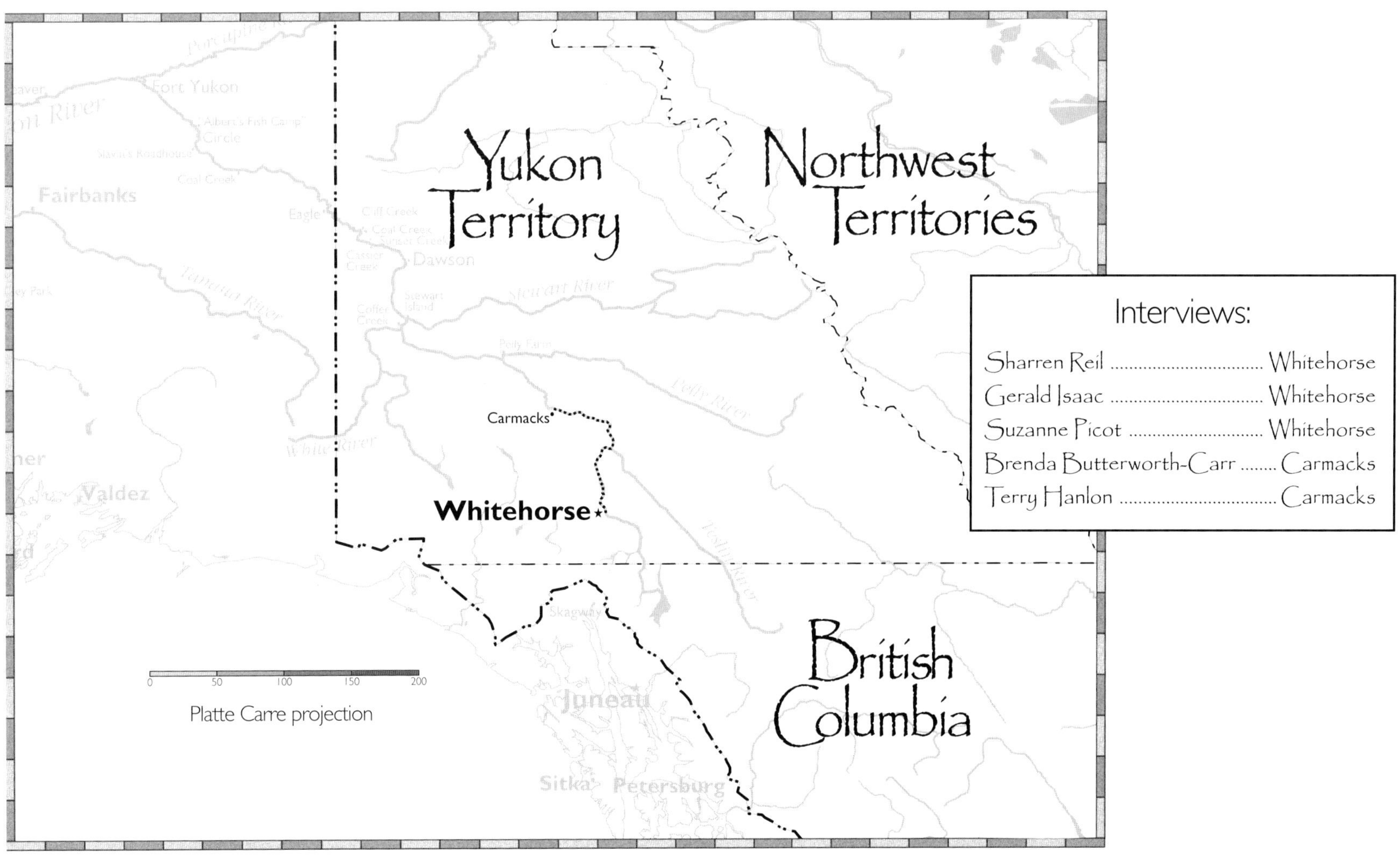
Yukon
Territory
Northwest
Territories
British
Columbia
Carmacks
Whitehorse
Dawson
Fort Yukon
Fairbanks
Valdez
Juneau
Sitka
Petersburg
0 50 100 150 200
Platte Carre projection
Interviews:
Sharren Reil .... Whitehorse
Gerald Isaac .... Whitehorse
Suzanne Picot .... Whitehorse
Brenda Butterworth-Carr .... Carmacks
Terry Hanlon .... Carmacks

After a short stint of tree planting to raise some extra cash, I arrive in Whitehorse a few days ahead of Kathleen. As soon as I get there, I call my friend Sharren. She is a redhead with inexhaustible energy whom I haven't seen for two years.

"MoNNNIIIIIIIIIIIIIIIIIIque!!!!!" she yells into the phone. "Where are you?"

We arrange to meet for lunch. Over soup, she says. "I'm getting married in three days to a man I've been engaged to for two weeks!" After lunch we drive through town in her Jeep and stop at a traffic light. She leaps out of the vehicle, runs over to some construction workers and yells, "I'm going to be a wife!!!"

When Kathleen arrives in Whitehorse, we set up our tent in the campground on the outskirts of town. A few days later, I bring Kathleen over to meet the glowing Sharren, who has agreed to be our first interview subject.

The long, hot afternoon flies by as Sharren, a born storyteller, tells us about her life in the Yukon. Then, when asked about the wedding she says, "It's going to be a simple ceremony at my cabin on Long Lake Road. I'm going to wear my black, gauzy dress and stand barefoot on a carpet of purple Lupines. Jon is going to wear his lucky tie."

We deliver our wedding gift on the morning of the big day: a three tiered cake blanketed in whipped cream and wildflowers.

"Wow! It's great!" Sharren says, clapping her hands. "Hey Jon! Check out the cake they made!"

After making a portrait of the newlyweds, I take pictures of Sharren galloping happily around the field in front of the cabin. The photos don't turn out, but it is a great wedding anyway. To me it is a fitting and lucky beginning to our trip.

The wedding is an entertaining distraction, but, once it is over, we have to get to work. Standing on the sidewalk the next morning in Whitehorse, we look for someone to interview. I feel ridiculous. After wandering around aimlessly for a while, we decide to go for coffee. Then, from the window of the restaurant, Kathleen sees a man with a long silver beard drive by on a low-slung motorcycle.

"Hey, Monique! What about him?" she asks excitedly.

Dressed from head to toe in black leather, the man would have been an imposing sight except for the human-sized teddy bear straddling the seat behind him. As he parks down the street, we agree to try him. Because I am nervous and don't really know what to say, I explain everything in excruciating detail: " . . . so then the Canada Council awarded a grant to do the project . . . "

The man, whose name is Leo McCormick, nods politely through my rambling monologue. Then, when I finally take a breath, he says, "So you want to interview me?"

"Yes!" Kathleen and I answer in unison.

Snapshots of people cover every surface of his small shack at the edge of town.

"I've got friends all over the world," he says, seeing us look at the walls.

When he goes to make us coffee, Kathleen points to a little sign by the door: DYING POOR IS SAD—DYING RICH IS STUPID! After Leo returns, we sit down and Kathleen sets the tape recorder on the cluttered coffee table.

She pushes the record button and says, "Whitehorse, Leo McCormick, June 8, 1993."

Born in Nova Scotia, Leo was in the merchant marine, fought in Korea, lived in Australia, was a longshoreman, worked in a sawmill in British Columbia, and walked from Halifax to Vancouver in 27 days, although he admits he took a few rides along the way.

"I lived so many lives by the time I was twenty," he says, "that I wouldn't have minded if I died."

Between Australia and British Columbia, Leo goes to fix us

something to eat. Kathleen and I look at each other. He truly had a remarkable past, but when was he going to get to the Yukon?

"Now, where was I?" he asks, handing each of us a huge plate of salad. He finally talks about the Yukon.

Later, as we drive back to town, I say, "Well, I think the interview was a success."

"You think so?" Kathleen asks. "I was just thinking how badly it went."

"No, I think it went well. We just have to remember to keep the interview focused on people's thoughts on the north."

Since starting our trip near the Yukon River's inaccessible, mountainous source isn't relevant to our trip's central purpose, I choose the convenience of beginning our voyage in Whitehorse, a few miles downriver instead. On June 15, after running into town to buy the last few essentials—magic markers and a bottle of Jameson's Irish Whisky—we start packing our mountain of gear into the 18' fiberglass canoe on Whitehorse's sandy riverfront. By five o'clock, we finally finish.

Exhausted, we are standing on the shore with Sharren and Jon, who have come to say their good-byes. Kathleen hands Sharren a magic marker and asks her to write something and to sign her name on the inside of the canoe. We plan to ask people we meet along the way to do the same. Sharren wades to the front of the boat and writes something on the outside.

"Hey Sharren!" I call out. "Write it on the inside or it'll wash away."

She has gotten as far as "My Heart"—before I stop her. The way she wrote it, following the curve of the prow, it is a perfect name for our boat. It never did wash away.

After hugs all around, Kathleen and I get into the boat and Sharren pushes us off. She and Jon wave from the shore as we pull into the current and head for the sea.

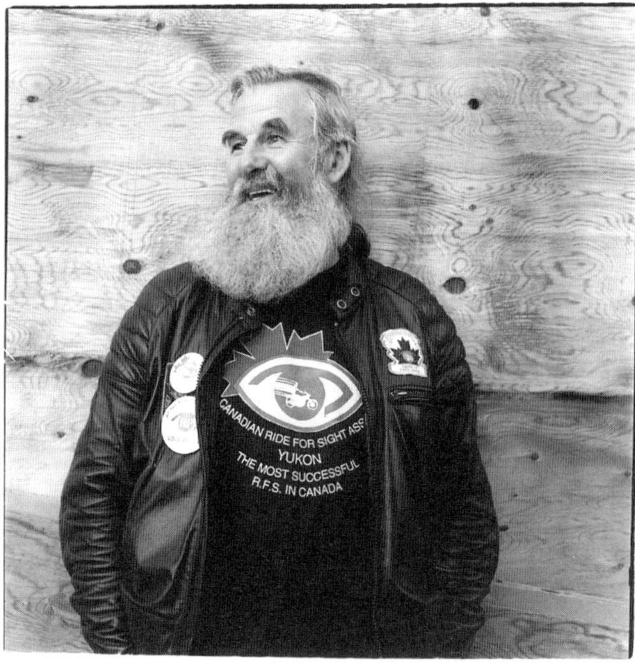

Leo McCormick

"My Heart" Milepost 202, Carmacks • *Terry's Frying Pan*

The derelict shacks lining Whitehorse's waterfront recede as we paddle into the hot, golden night. The boat cuts heavily through the sun tipped waves as steep, sandy banks fly by. I glance back and see that Sharren and Jon are gone.

"Kathleen! We did it!" I say. "We actually left!"

"Miraculous!" she replies, not missing a paddle stroke.

The canoe's load is lopsided and my arms soon ache with the effort of keeping the boat upright. "Break time?" I say an hour later, my clenched arm muscles prickly and hot.

"I'm sure ready for one," sighs Kathleen, stretching her arms and tilting her head towards the sky.

I stretch out my legs on a canoe pack and stare gloomily at my shoelaces. At leaving, I thought I'd feel excitement, a swell of pride and great satisfaction at realizing my dream. Instead, I'm tense and anxious and wonder why we are here.

The sun still shines brightly at 9:30 p.m. when we stop on a little island for the night. We go exploring before unloading the boat. Tall trees ring a well trampled clearing. At the clearing's edge, we follow a small path that leads to a large, white teepee.

"There's nothing inside except an old fire," Kathleen says, pushing the door flap aside. "Hey! Lets sleep here tonight!"

I build a fire in the teepee while Kathleen makes supper. After big plates of spaghetti, we wash the dishes and store the gear under the canoe.

"Teepee?" Kathleen says, draping her wet tea towel over a stump.

"Yeah!" I answer, abandoning a burnt pot.

Like parentheses, we curl around a cheery little fire and watch the sparks whirl up through the dark circle of sky at the top of the teepee. Kathleen says goodnight after flicking her cigarette into the fire. Drifting off, I remember my earlier panic and smile. I was wrong, this was a great idea.

We hit patches of rain and squall the next day on the Yukon River's Lake Laberge. Kathleen, kneeling in the bow, paddles strongly while I attempt to steer from the stern. As the canoe crashes through the waves, we struggle past mountains, inlets, and long empty beaches. Suddenly the wind stops and the lake becomes a glassy mirror, reflecting the clouds and sky. The boat is briefly enveloped in a silver-blue, horizonless world. We stop paddling.

The smooth, unbroken water reminds me of a Han Indian legend: "A long time ago, there was no land and water flowed all over the world. There was one family and they lived on a big raft with all kinds of animals. The man of the family tied a rope around a beaver and sent him down to find the bottom, but he only got halfway before he drowned. The man then tied a string around a muskrat and sent him down. The muskrat reached bottom, but, after getting a little mud in his claws, he also drowned. The man took the mud out of the muskrat's claws, let it dry in his palm, then crumbled it into dust. Blowing the dust out over the water, he made the land."[1]

Lake Laberge's notoriously tempestuous wind soon rises and we have to start paddling again.

"What's that red thing up there?" asks Kathleen a few minutes later, pointing to a tiny speck in the waves with her dripping paddle. Some time later, a young man in a kayak cheerily waves his paddle when we pass him tossing awkwardly on the waves.

A few days later, we meet this paddler, named Hiroshi, in Carmacks.

"I'm going to visit the grave of Jack Yashuda in Beaver, Alaska," he says shyly, then continues, "that's about 900 miles from here."

At the turn of the century, Jack Yashuda apparently led a group of Eskimos from Alaska's desolate north coast to a new life along the Yukon River at Beaver. Hiroshi washed dishes at a steak restaurant in Vancouver for two years to save up for this trip. Then, after buying the best kayak money could buy, he'd spent the rest of his savings on supplies and a one-way bus ticket to Whitehorse.

"I'd never been in a kayak before I left Whitehorse," he quietly confides.

The next morning we wave good-bye, and then watch Hiroshi's kayak disappear down the dark river.

"What an unbelievable guy," Kathleen says, a mixture of disbelief and awe in her voice. "I hope he finds what he's looking for."

Terry Hanlon found what he was looking for—an old fashioned life—at Dadzo Ranch. We visit the hodgepodge of buildings a few miles downriver from Carmacks, several hours after waving Hiroshi off.

"And how are ya, darlin'?" says Terry, a warm smile on his narrow, freckled face. He is an old friend from Forestry. "And who is your friend?" he asks, looking at Kathleen with considerable interest.

Knowing Terry's romantic nature, I say, "This is Kathleen. Don't you fall in love with her now!" Laughing, Terry thumps my arm then asks, "What are you doing here?"

We tell him about the trip and ask if he would like to be interviewed.

"Sure, why not?" he says.

After the interview, Terry prepares for his photograph by tossing his everyday hat onto a chair and, after smoothing his ginger colored hair, he carefully dons his good hat. I look closely, but both dusty, squashed brimmed leather cowboy hats seem identical. "Stay for supper?" Terry asks when we're done.

"As long as you let us do the dishes," Kathleen answers.

"Deal!" he says.

Still early, Terry and I go horseback riding while Kathleen stays behind to read a book. Dodging low branches on a cream colored horse, I follow Terry through the pine forest at the edge of his property. Ahead of me, shirtless and back in his everyday hat, Terry sings tunelessly as his horse threads its way through the trees. Slapping his leg in time to the music, a small dust cloud erupting whenever his hand hits his jeans, he looks like a completely contented man.

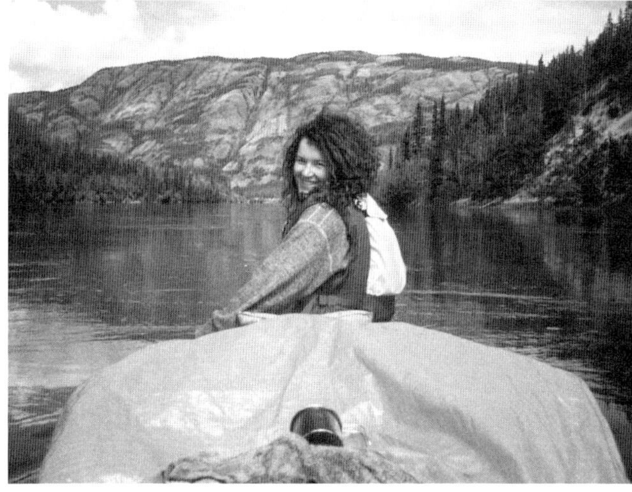

Kathleen Usher

He doesn't look quite as content that evening. While Kathleen washes the dinner plates, I struggle for a long time over a large, greasy cast iron frying pan.

"Oh my god! You *wrecked* it!" he says in a strangled voice, seeing the pan neatly inverted on the dish rack. "Never—never—never—*never* wash cast iron pots with soap! That pan is over five years old and it's never been washed before!"

---

[1] Claire Fejes, *Villagers, Athabaskan Indian Life along the Yukon River* (New York: Random House, 1981), p. 171.

June 9

Sharren Reil
Whitehorse, YT

Sharren was born in 1959 and raised in Victoria, British Columbia. She studied Human Resources in college, then worked with severely retarded people. She arrived in the Yukon in 1987 and spent three years in the Dawson area, living in a remote bush cabin with a friend. In 1991, Sharren moved to Whitehorse where she works with handicapped adults. The photograph is of her and her groom, Jon Breen, on their wedding day.

Talking bears

I had decided that this was it. I was going to stay and do a winter up here. Then me and Sebastian got together. We got offered a dog team and an intensely beautiful log cabin. Winter adventure, take one. We make coffee, I'm smoking a cigarette and all of a sudden, at the same moment, we both look at each other and it's like "What am I doing? Who is this person?" You're locked into a winter together. You know it's going to be 40 below. All your money has gone into supplies for the winter and you're sitting across the table looking at this person. You have no idea who this person truly is and you're in a cabin in the middle of nowhere with him!

I was so in love with the north that winter, I mean, almost beyond comprehension. Everything was magical. Ice crystals made me bounce. Northern lights made me stoned out of my mind.

I had this romantic image of what living on the land would be like. What I didn't realize was how brutal it also was. You're on a caribou hunt and there's blood on the snow and fresh guts steaming in your hands. It was hideous. Then you'd look and you'd see hoar frost on the trees in the sunshine and it would be one of the most beautiful things you'd ever seen in your entire life. It would delight your soul. It was constantly like that in the bush. Beautiful. Brutal. Beautiful. Brutal. You began to realize that you couldn't put your preconceived notions on the land. It wasn't a Walt Disney film on any level and the bears weren't going to talk to you. It just was.

Swimming naked in the dog yard

We were down at Cliff Creek one year in the spring. Six o'clock in the morning, I hear my dogs screaming. I jump up out of bed. The river had broken, then the ice jammed. The dog yard was flooding! The dogs were screaming. My dogs were up to their necks in water and it was still rising! "SEBASTIAN!" We go running out naked. We've got 19 dogs chained up. The first dog I come to is a bitch that had three puppies. She's got one puppy in her mouth and the other two are gone. Water is moving. It's really really cold and there's ice in it. This dog, she's going to drown before she loses that baby. I grabbed the baby, run back to shore, put the baby down, unchain the bitch. We've got to let all these dogs loose before they drown. There was one dog whose chain was so tangled. Who knows what happened. We get all the dogs turned loose except for this one dog. And we're swimming now. We're swimming in the water. We can't get the chain undone. Sebastian swims back and grabs the gun. He shoots the dog so it doesn't have to drown. The second he shot it, the water stopped rising.

It's a grand adventure. Everything. It's a grand adventure.

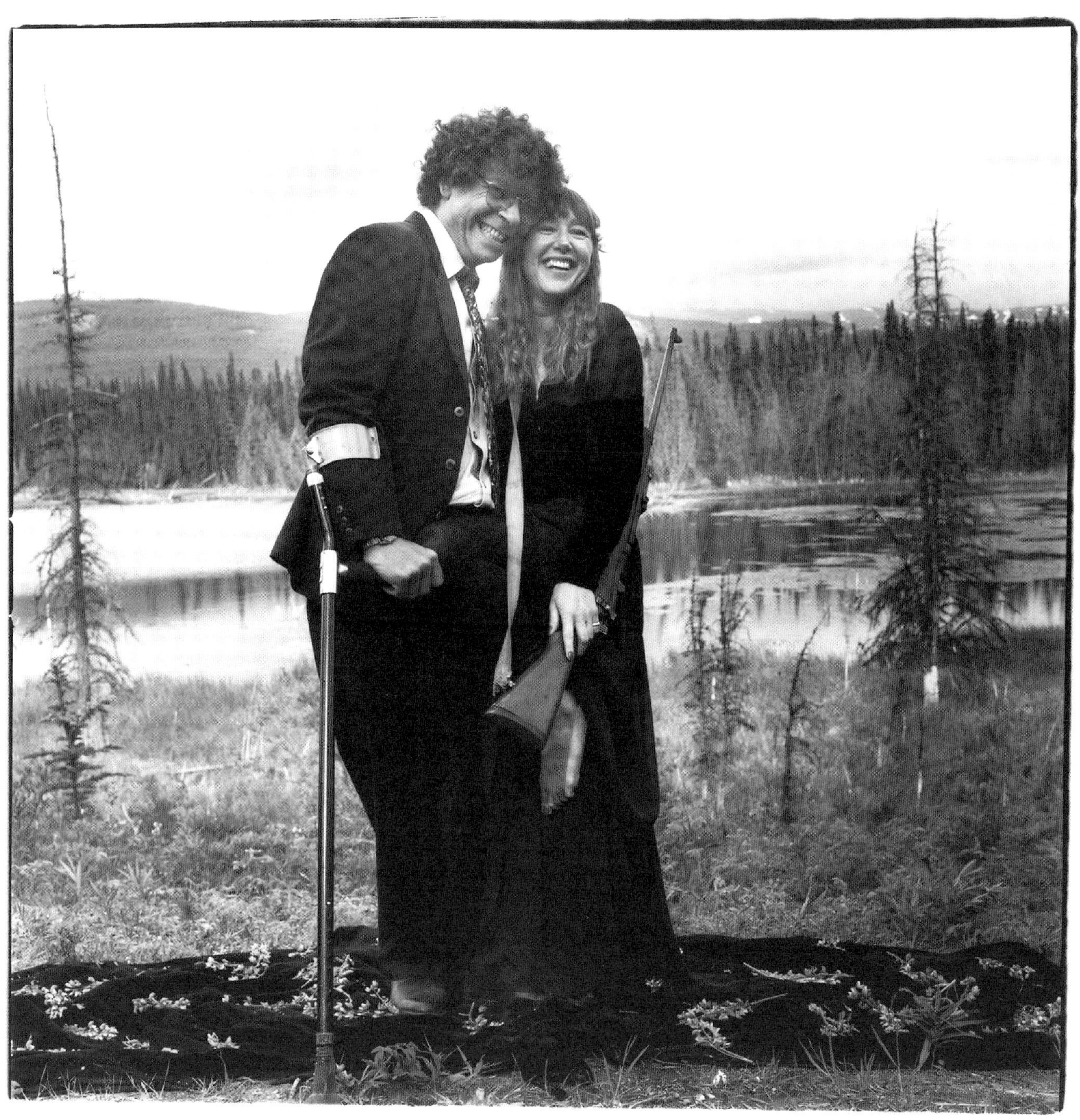

Born in Dawson, Gerald was raised by his grandmother. At 16, he moved to Whitehorse to study drafting, then worked as a civil engineer for the next 15 years. After serving as a Yukon land claims negotiator for several years after that, Gerald became the Director of the Aboriginal Language Service for the Yukon government, where he has worked for the last four years. Gerald and his wife have three adopted children.

June 11

Gerald Isaac
Whitehorse, YT

Boundaries

Our people were nomadic. In the fall time, we would get our meat, pick berries, and prepare for winter. In the summer time, we'd catch king salmon coming up the river. Our people never recognized political boundaries. Neither did the river, for that matter, nor the salmon or the wild animals that occupied either side of the present-day boundary.

When the international boundary was put in between Alaska and the Yukon, our people on both sides of the boundary held a mourning potlatch. There was major fear that families would be separated forever. And it happened. Even today, I'm still trying to locate lost relations on the Alaska side. Recently, though, I attended a Han gathering in Eagle, Alaska. It was the first time in 86 years that this has happened.

His grandfather's song

You either use your language or you lose it. If you lose your language, you lose your culture, your traditions, and your whole identity. Language and culture are one. You cannot separate them. You cannot. When I wake up in the morning, the first words that come to me are in Han. I teach my granddaughter, but I have no one to talk to. When I get really lonesome, I call up one of the elders in Dawson and talk to them.

I want to learn my grandfather's song. I want to sing it, drum it, and to dance to it so that one day I'll be able to bring that song back to the Han territory in the Yukon.

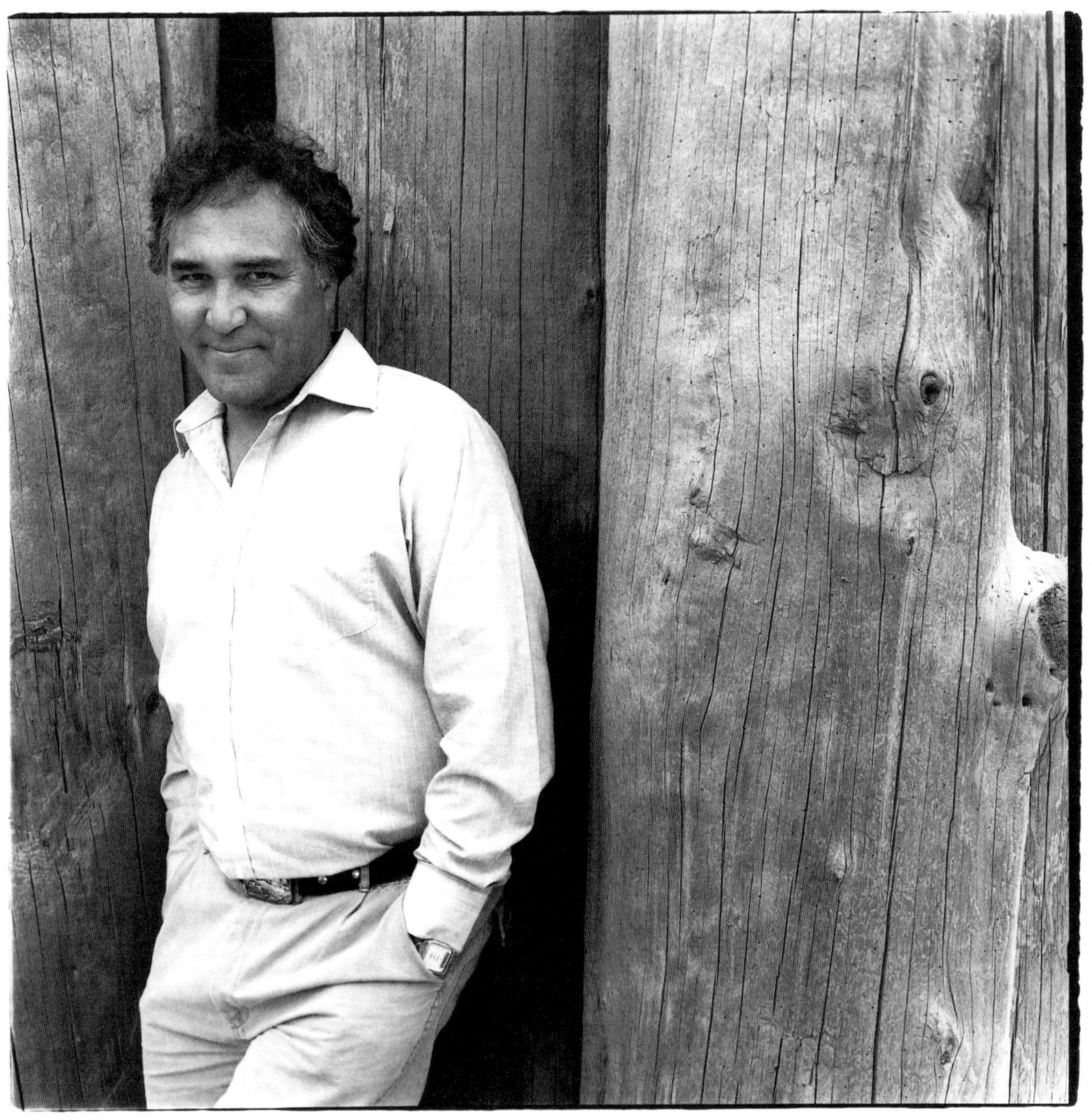

Suzanne was born in 1960 in Bathurst, New Brunswick. She married a local boy at the age of 19. Soon after the wedding, the young couple moved to Haines Junction, Yukon Territory. After quite a few years of marriage, the couple amicably separated. When we met Suzanne, she was a social worker in Whitehorse and drove a Toyota station wagon that looked like a cow.

June 14

Suzanne Picot
Whitehorse, YT

The right doilies

When I was married, I had the complete eight piece setting of the Royal Dalton china. That was quite something. Now I only have two plates that match. That's my ultimate goal. To not have any plates, any cups, anything that match. They all have to be very different. Because when I was married, I wasn't a complete woman if I didn't have a complete set of china. Scary, eh? So much energy is consumed in finding the right doilies to match your silverware.

This is a place that forces you to face your fears. It's kind of a challenge to see how you're going to deal with the things that aren't part of your nice, pink, fluffy world, you know? The nice comfort zone. Because it's very scary to step beyond the norm. It's frightening. You have to rely on your own resilience. Your own resourcefulness.

The following is an excerpt of a letter from Suzanne, dated November 9, 1994

I've found the connection to the whole cow thing. Remember, I had no idea why I HAD to paint my car that way? Well, I met a man and fell in love with him and guess what? He grew up on a dairy farm! He sent me a picture of Martha, his favorite cow and she looks just like my car. Now, is that a bizarre/karmic thing or what? I now drive a beige station wagon with vines all over it.

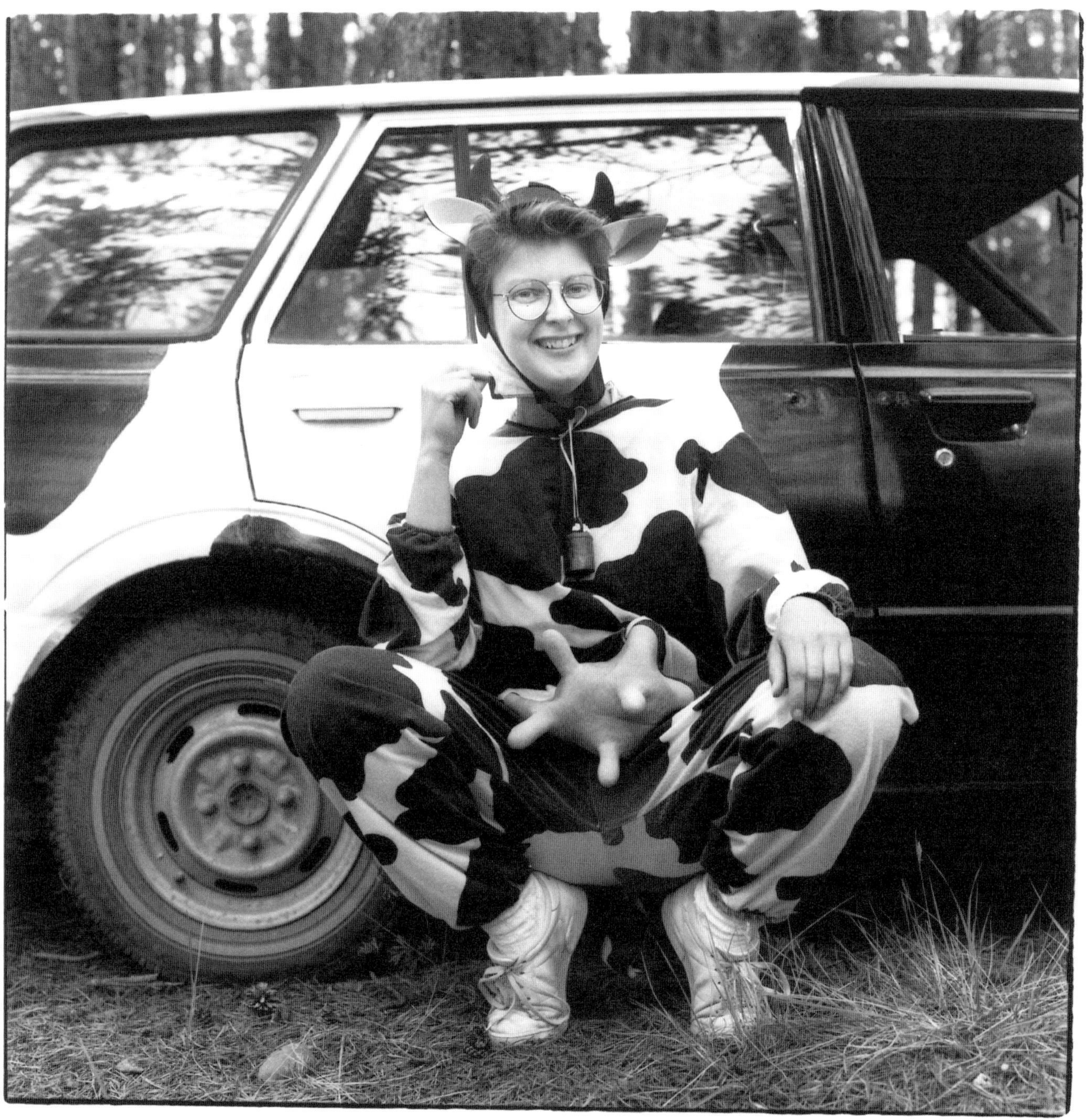

June 24

Brenda Butterworth-Carr
Carmacks, YT

Brenda was born and raised in Dawson. At the age of 22, she married her high school sweetheart. The mother of two sons, Brenda is an R.C.M.P. officer presently stationed in Carmacks.

What she is

I plan on leaving the Yukon in about five years to go to Alberta and continue with police work down there. But I know I'm going to come home and I'm going to retire here. You can take the person out of the Yukon, but you can't take the Yukon out of the person. And that's how I feel. When I'm away, I miss it. I miss the environment. I miss the people. I just have a sense of belonging. I haven't felt that anywhere except for here. This is what I am.

You're Canadian

[We were] raised as a white family, but then I started to find this whole new other culture that I really like. I'm proud of both sides of mine. As far as I'm concerned, the more cultures you participate in, the better off you'll be. You should be proud of who you are. You're Canadian and that's what you should be proud of, whether white or native or whatever.

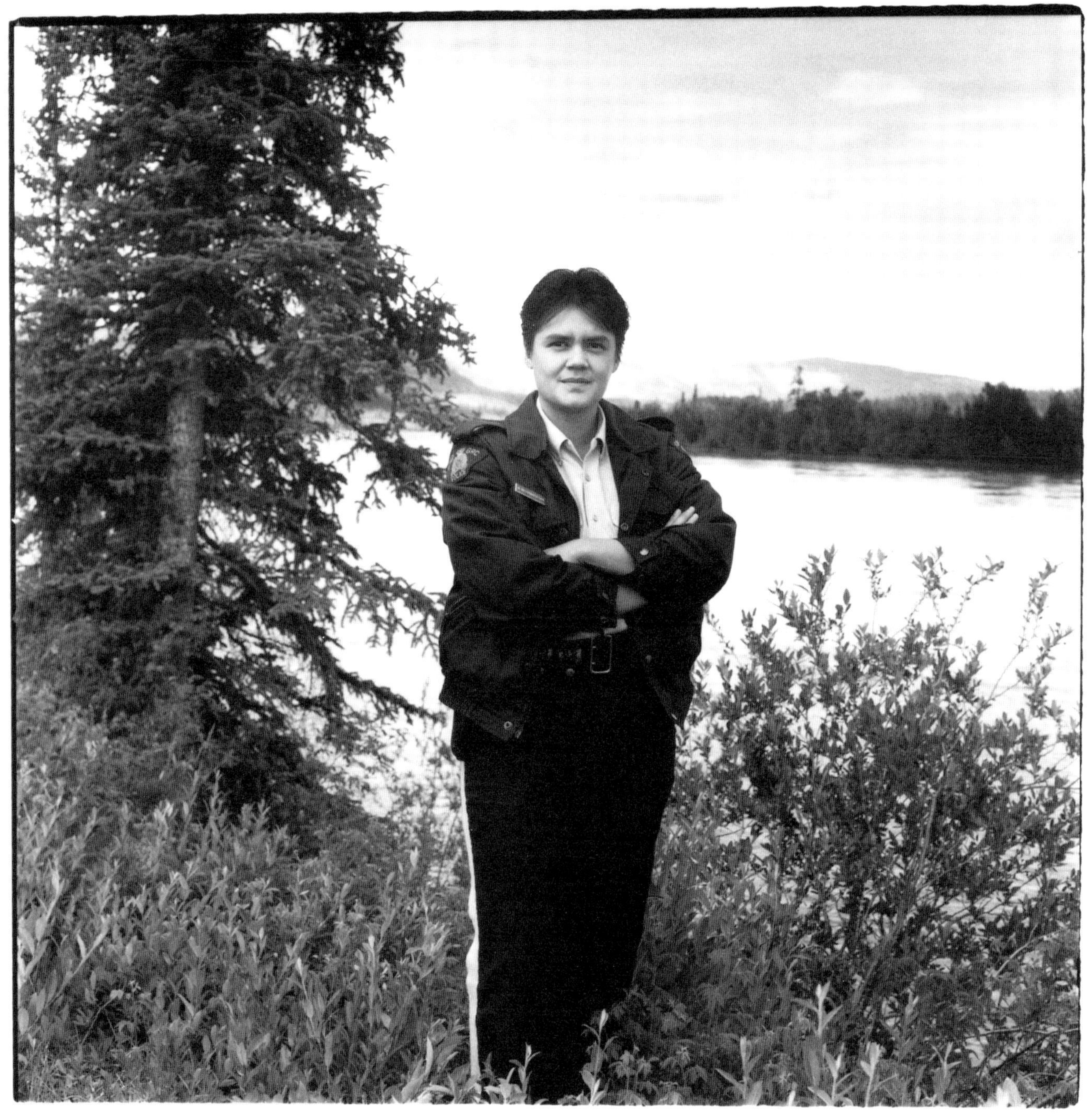

June 26

Terry Hanlon
Carmacks, YT

Terry was born in 1946 in Stratford, Ontario. After a year of university, he traveled to western Canada and took a variety of jobs. In 1976, Terry moved to the Yukon. In the north, he has worked as a wilderness guide, logger, heavy equipment operator, and for the Department of Forestry. In 1986, he bought some land outside Carmacks and started Dadzo Ranch. Terry hopes to have the ranch completed within the next ten years.

Open arms

When I started hanging out in Carmacks, the native people opened up their arms and just enveloped me . . . they were warm and generous and welcoming. That's one thing about the native culture—anyone who is willing to adopt their ways is just brought in . . . nobody could ever freeze or starve to death around here.

Living old fashioned

I find it really great to be able to not be part of the modern world. To be kind of old fashioned. To live, you need a nice warm, dry place. You need food from time to time. It's out there, you just have to go and get it. There's moose and caribou and rabbits. Squirrels. Porcupine. All sorts of herbs and plant life. You go fish salmon when it comes up the river to spawn, and grayling and whitefish. You plant a big garden and weed and water it. All your needs are supplied by the land, more or less. All you have to buy is flour and tea, salt, and sugar. A person needs very little to live really comfortable in this country.

Cavalry charge

I wish I had a trumpet. My trumpet got broke when I was riding on a horse. I was carrying it around, playing the post parade and the cavalry charge and stuff, just trying to keep my lip up. I really miss it.

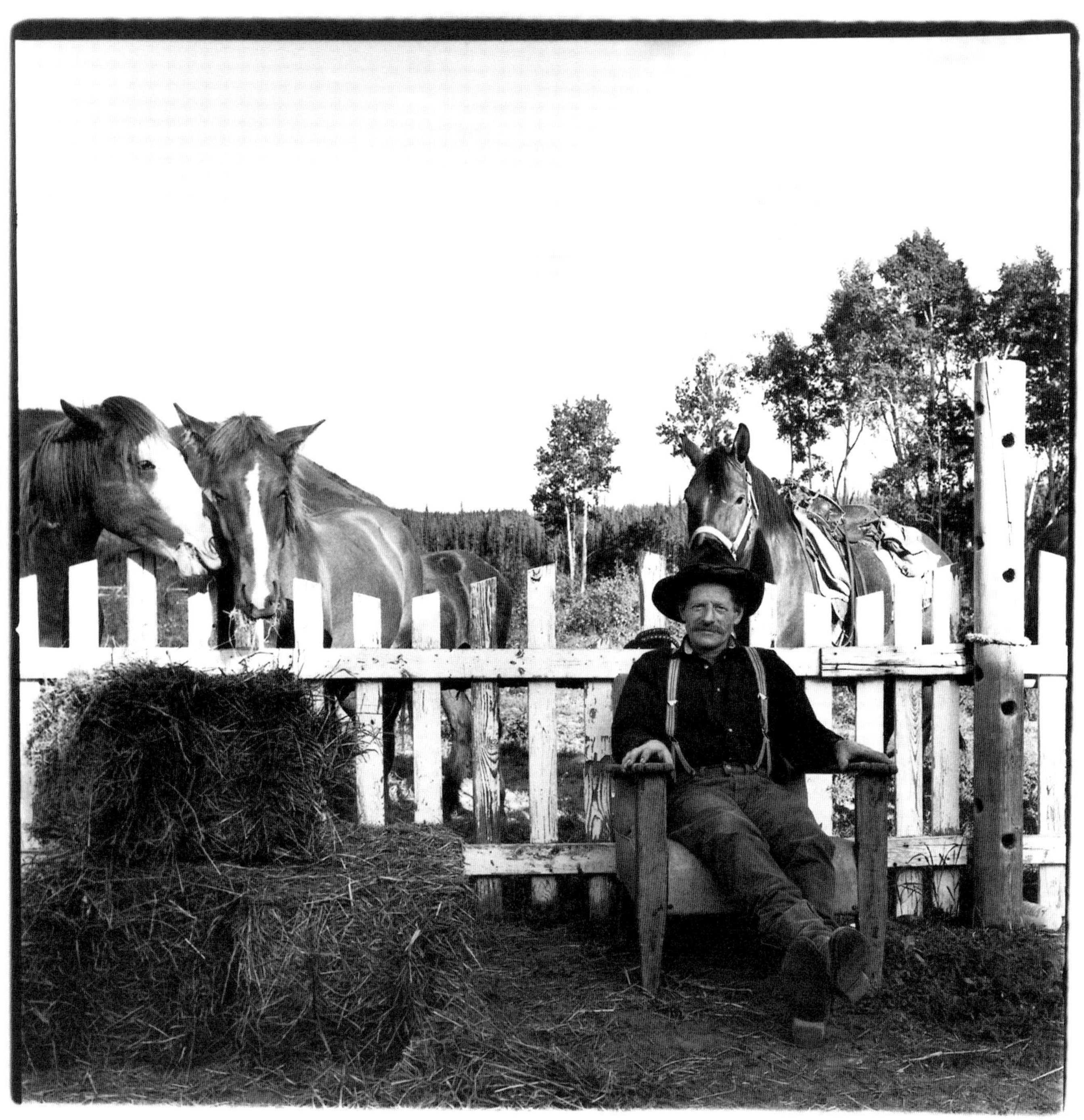

Carmacks to Coal Creek, Yukon Territory

"My Heart" Milepost 460, Dawson • *The Snake Pit*

As we pack the boat at Coffee Creek, Debbie Degraaf writes "God Bless You" in curly writing on the bottom of the canoe.

"Good-bye! Good luck! God bless!" she yells from shore, her voice a thin whisper in the wind.

I look back and see she is waving good-bye with broad sweeps of her arm, her children as thick as rabbits around her legs.

"I guess God really does send lots of people to Coffee Creek," I say as we pull into the swiftly moving current.

Just short of 2,000 miles long, the Yukon River is the fifth largest river system in North America. The watershed covers part of British Columbia, the southern three-quarters of Yukon Territory, and much of Alaska—an area of 325,000 square miles. Its icy, glacier-fed headwaters begin in a cluster of lakes near the northern border of British Columbia, less than 20 miles from salt water at Lynn Canal. With each additional tributary, it soon becomes a wide, fast river. Through the Yukon Flats in Alaska, the river is wide and sluggish, but, near Rampart, it flows quickly again between steep, forested banks. Below Tanana, the remaining 800 miles flows through a broad, swampy, lake-covered delta. Then, near the mouth, the river takes an abrupt turn to the north and empties into Norton Sound, an arm of the Bering Sea.

Called Youcon (White Water River) by some natives and Yu-kun-ah (Great River)[1] by others, it is navigable from its mouth almost to its source, providing a transportation route into the interior, much like Canada's other great northern river, the Mackenzie. Unlike the St. Lawrence, the Yukon has no large rapids to restrict travel and commerce, other than the Five Finger and Rink rapids near Whitehorse. This was fortunate since most of my canoeing experience was on northern Ontario's more placid lakes and rivers.

From the late 1800s until after the Alaska Highway was built in the 1940s, river steamers and paddlewheelers were a common sight on the river. In recent decades, the river's Whitehorse to Dawson stretch has gained in popularity for recreational canoeing and kayaking. It took us more than two weeks to cover this distance, before rounding a long bend in the river above Dawson on a scorchingly hot afternoon in early July.

"Is that Dawson up there?" Kathleen asks, pointing to a small, multicolored jumble of houses on the riverbank.

"No way. It's still miles away," I say with groggy authority from the stern where, instead of paddling, I am watching a wispy cloud disintegrate into the pale blue sky. Then I do a double take. "Hey—you're right it is!" I say, grabbing my paddle. "Yahoo! Ice cold beer at the Pit! Boy—Dawson doesn't look like much from the river, eh?"

Both in history and in my memory, the town is far larger. During the Klondike gold rush of 1897-98, Dawson was briefly the greatest of frontier cities, its population swelling from 500 to 30,000. However, much of the richest land was staked long before most of the gold seekers arrived and, by the summer of 1898, people were leaving as quickly as they had arrived. The relatively few people who remained lived within the skeleton of the hastily assembled, then abandoned, city.

"Even the dead left here must now be lonesome," Ales Hrdlicka thought after seeing the town in the 1920s.[2]

Recently, much time and money has gone into restoring the town to its turn-of-the-century authenticity. "Heritage" buildings have been disassembled, rebuilt, then painted a rainbow of colors, turning the town into a garish kind of monument.

"To the Pit!" I say after we set the tent up. It has been two years since I've been to Dawson, and I can't wait to see familiar faces. As we open the door, a sharp triangle of light stretches across the worn linoleum floor. The faded blue curtains, drawn against the sun, emit a watery glow.

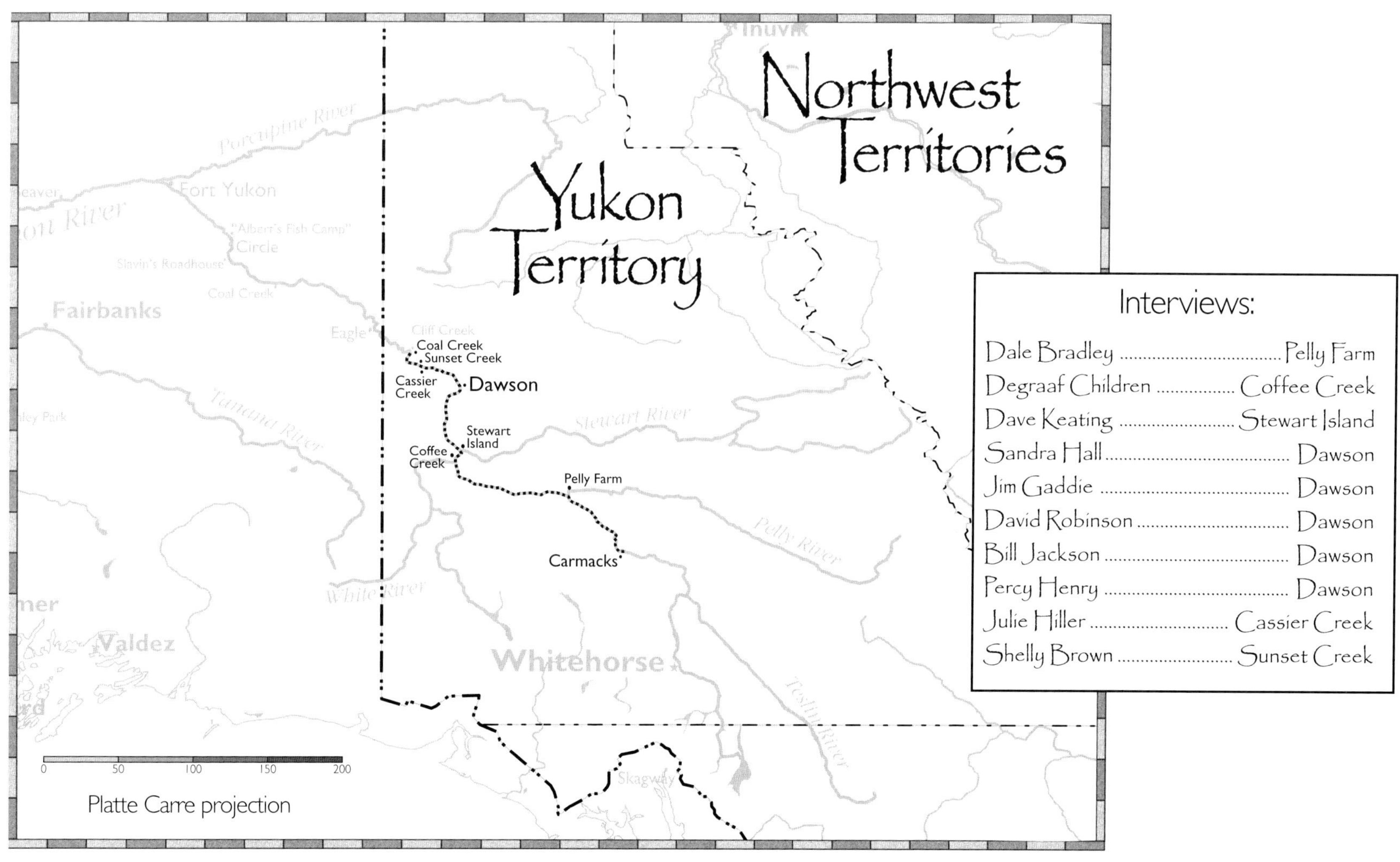
Northwest Territories
Yukon Territory
Fort Yukon
"Albert's Fish Camp"
Circle
Slavin's Roadhouse
Coal Creek
Fairbanks
Eagle
Cliff Creek
Coal Creek
Sunset Creek
Cassier Creek
Dawson
Stewart Island
Coffee Creek
Pelly Farm
Carmacks
Porcupine River
Tanana River
Stewart River
Pelly River
White River
Teslin River
Valdez
Whitehorse
Skagway
0 50 100 150 200
Platte Carre projection
Interviews:
Dale Bradley .... Pelly Farm
Degraaf Children .... Coffee Creek
Dave Keating .... Stewart Island
Sandra Hall .... Dawson
Jim Gaddie .... Dawson
David Robinson .... Dawson
Bill Jackson .... Dawson
Percy Henry .... Dawson
Julie Hiller .... Cassier Creek
Shelly Brown .... Sunset Creek

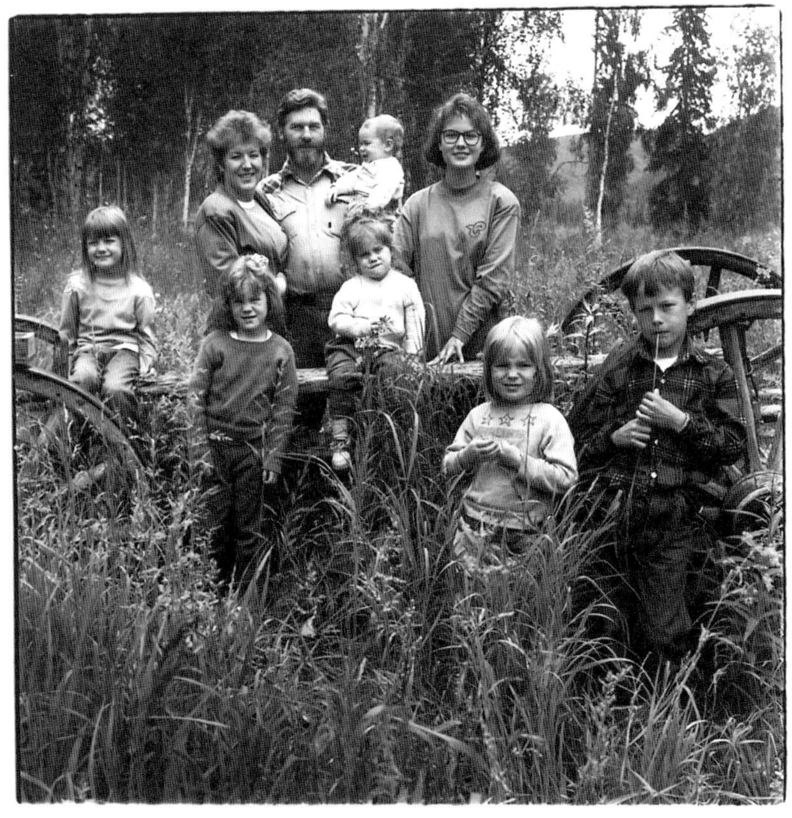

Degraaf family

"Hey, Mo-*nique*! Long time no see!" Eric Nelson's pleasant face is split by a grin as he envelopes me in a bony hug. "Nice to see yah! Buy yah a drink?"

This *is* a special day, I think, as I introduce Kathleen.

Soon, Eric appears with three sweating draught beers and we sit at a table by the door. Everything is the same—the chipped arborite bar, the loud, drunken voices, the jukebox spewing indecipherable music from the corner. We stay until midnight, as the light shining through a crack in the curtains gradually turns a deep orange. Kathleen's wide, beery grin mirrors the giddy joy I feel as we stumble back to our tent in the soft tangerine twilight.

Because I know so many people in Dawson, it is easy to find subjects to interview. Bill Jackson, his Scots kilt whipping around his legs, poses for me on a hilltop—with the river a silver thread below. He plays the bagpipes as I unpack my camera gear. Excited by what a beautiful photograph this will be, I grab a roll of film and load it into the camera. It jams! I pull the film out and grab another roll. It jams as well! The wind and cold heighten the panic I am starting to feel.

Bill stops playing and says, "Are you almost finished yet? I'm freezing!"

"Just about!" I say, grabbing the spare camera. After loading it successfully, I get a few shots before Bill says he's had enough. I later realize that in my excitement I tried to load two exposed rolls of film into the camera.

I see David the day before we leave. I haven't seen him in two years. Dressed in army surplus clothing, his face is pale and drawn. I am in the Snake Pit's parking lot, leaning against the hot pink wall when he walks by.

"Sure is windy on the river today," he says before disappearing into the Pit's murky interior.

I never see or speak to him again.

---

[1] Kenneth S. Coates and William Morrison, *Land of the Midnight Sun: A History of the Yukon* (Edmonton: Hurtig, 1988), p. 22.

[2] Ales Hrdlicka, *Alaska Diary, 1926-1931* (Lancaster, PA: Jacques Cattell, 1943), p. 158. Ales Hrdlicka (1869-1943) was a prominent scholar in North American archaeology and anthropology.

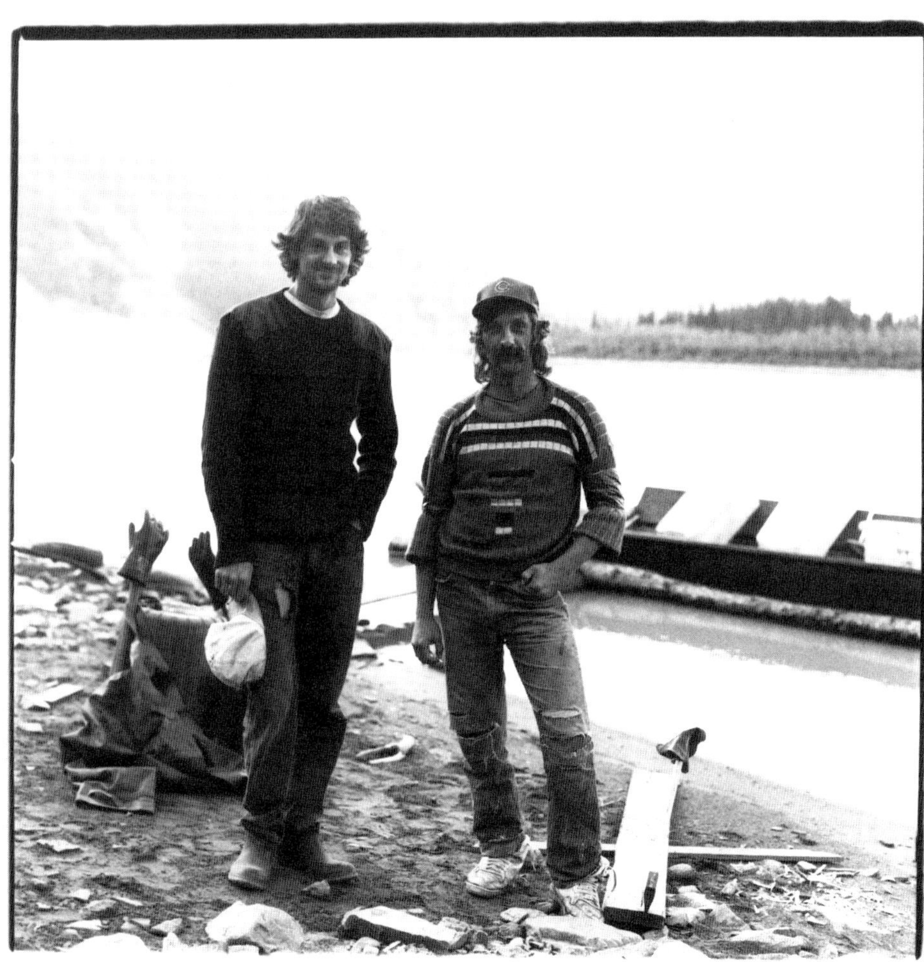

Eric Nelson and Frank Buck, at fish camp.

June 27

Dale Bradley
Pelly Farm, YT

Dale was born in 1961 and raised in Whitehorse. As a young man, he became a heavy equipment operator and worked in mining and road construction. In 1990, Dale became a farmer when he bought his uncle Dick's share of the family farm. Scattered around Pelly Farm are farming implements dating back to the turn of the century. Many are still in use.

The challenge

I phoned up a guy in Edmonton. That's the closest parts dealer. I told him I needed this and this and this.

He looked in his book and he says, "Well, they don't make these parts any more. You know that seed drill? If you don't mind me saying so, it's kind of old. Don't you think you could upgrade it a little?"

I says, "You know, I think you're right." I says "Next time I go by my local equipment dealer, I'll just pop in and pick one up."

He says, "Where's your local equipment dealer?"

I says, "Well, you're probably it."

He says "Well, how far away is that."

I says, "1,200 hundred miles."

Now, I could go out and get a new air seeder. And sure, it would be wonderful. I could get the tractor hammering down the field and get those seeds in the ground and be all done. But what happens if it breaks? You gotta think that way all the time. You gotta be able to fix what you got. That's part of the challenge of being here.

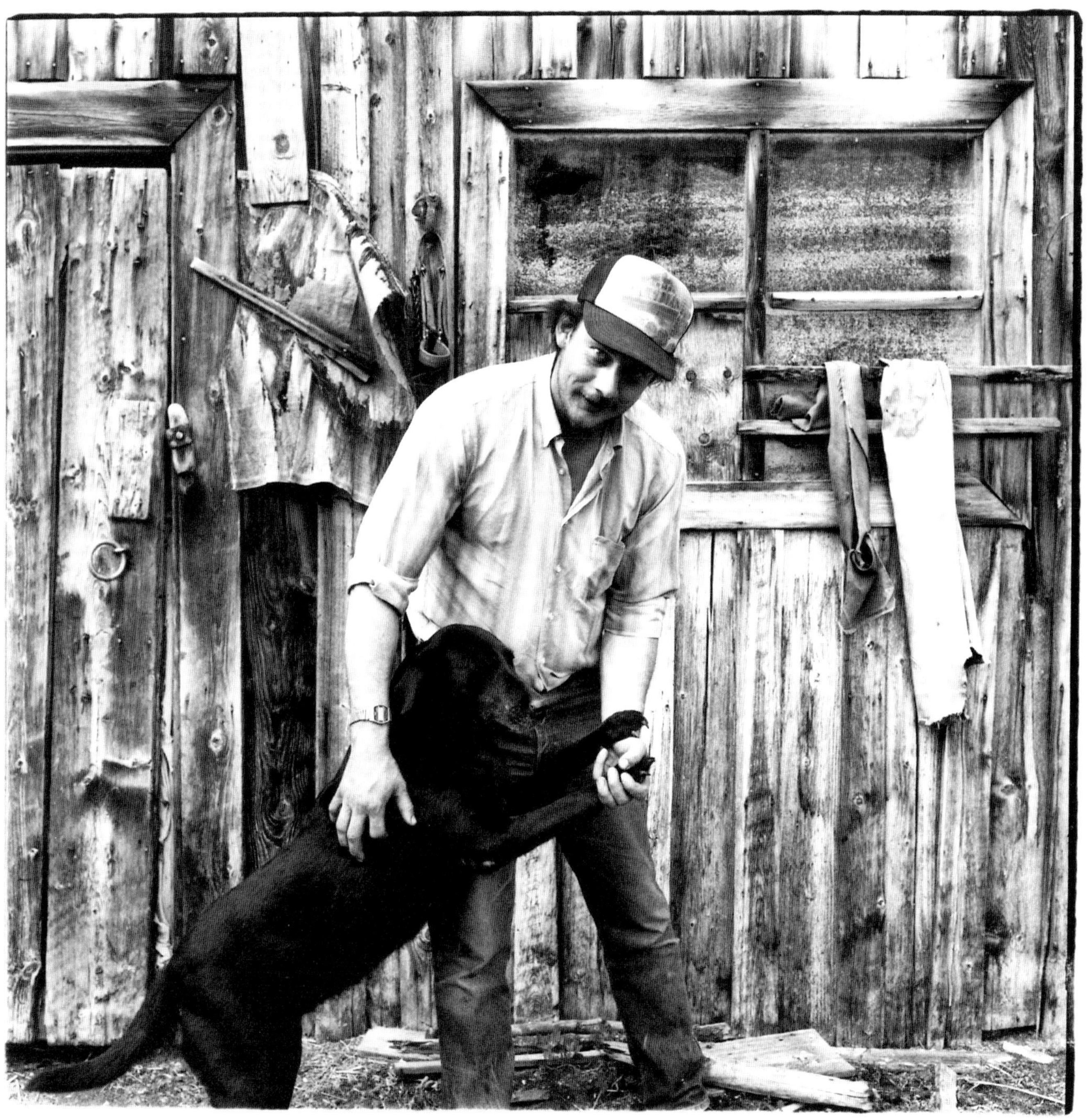

July 1

Degraaf Children
Coffee Creek, YT

Rick Degraaf was a pastoral counselor in Grand Rapids, Michigan, before he and his wife, Debbie, moved with their seven children to Coffee Creek, Yukon Territory. Sight unseen, they bought a trapper's cabin on a lonely stretch of the Yukon River. The family arrived in May 1990. We interviewed Debbie Degraaf at the new family home.

Their new home

O.K., so it's a cabin. I was expecting at least to move into a house that had a kitchen. Or a sink. I knew there was an outhouse. Does it have closets? What does the kitchen look like? Does it have a sink? Where's the sink? How many cupboards does it have? Then when I saw this place, I thought, "My lord, my chicken coop looks better than this!"

The one thing that really did us in, you know, was the water when we first came here. We didn't want the kids to get anything. So we were boiling everything. I could not keep up with boiling water. I mean, here I am with this propane tank trying to get the water to boil for ten minutes. Well then, the kids can't drink hot water, so it's got to cool off. We were always running out of water that first summer. I mean, I could hardly keep up with bread making let alone boiling water. "DON'T DRINK!! ARGUGH!" It was terrible. We were trying to get a garden in so I could have vegetables for the first winter.

My mother writes a letter: "Where's the glamour girl of Grand Rapids?" My hands are black. I'm going to choke my kids—they're drinking all the water. I come in to get something to eat and there's no bread left 'cause they've eaten it all . . . Frustrating. It was the most frustrating summer of my whole life!

The big flash Halleluia

We have changed. The way we look. The way we think about things. Our whole outlook on life, actually. Changed. In the United States, you work, work, work. For what? And you go, go, go. For what? I can see now what it is to be really effective as a Christian. It's not the way we were. Brand new cars, nice houses, nice clothes. The big flash Halleluia. That is not it! No! No! No! No! No! What I think, honestly, is that as a Christian, you have to do what the Lord wants you to do. Now, here, the Lord wanted maybe to humble us. For whatever reason.

The river

I think that river affects our lives in just one way. It allows God to bring just who he wants here. We figure the people that do stop are the ones God wants here.

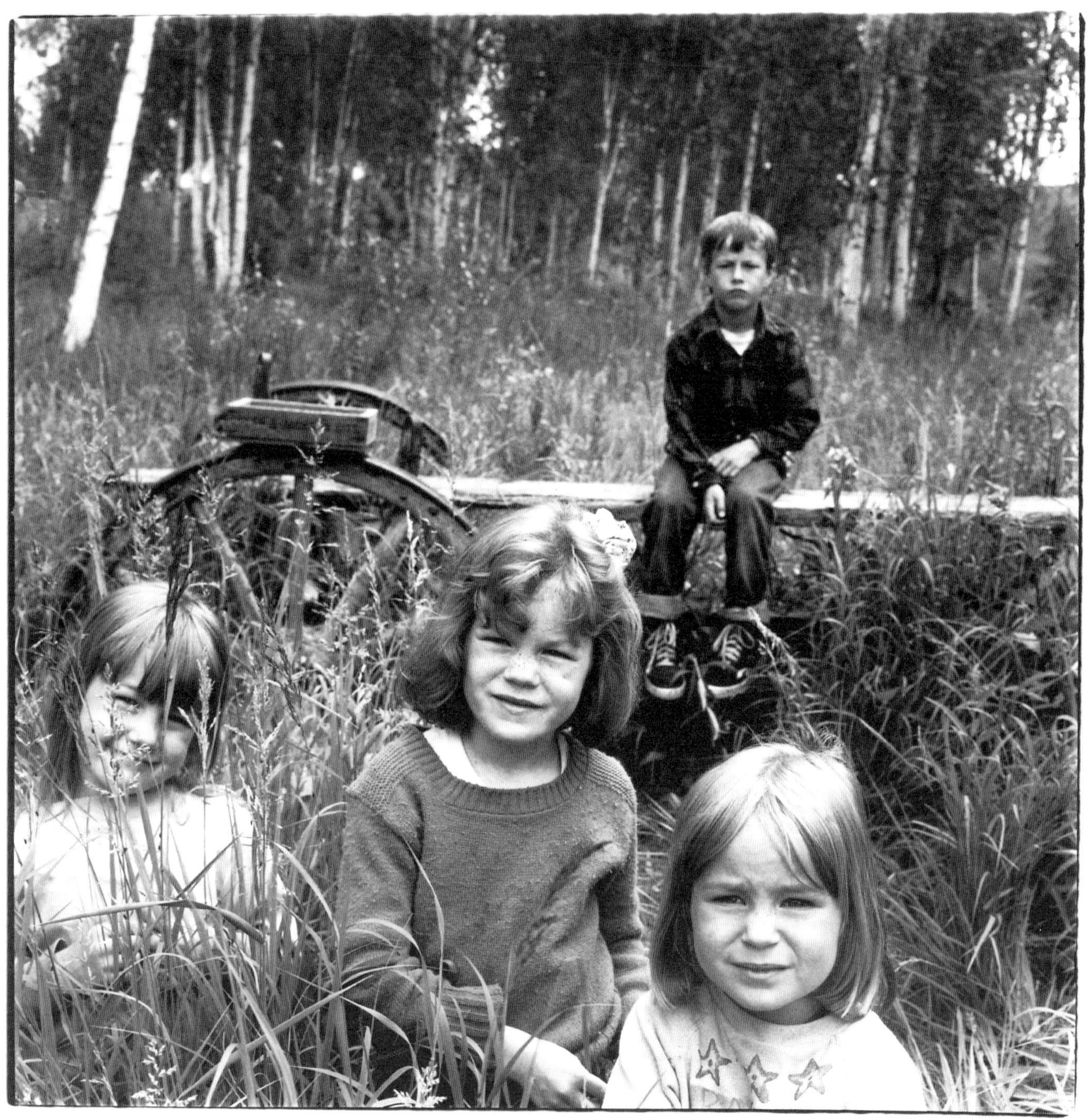

July 2

Dave Keating
Stewart Island, YT

Dave was born in Woodstock, Ontario, in 1943. At age 15, he left home to join the merchant marine. At 17, he became a long distance trucker. Trucking has been his most frequent profession, but he has had many jobs. Dave first arrived in the Yukon in 1970. We met him at Stewart Island where he was working as a caretaker for an elderly woman.

Hoeing your own row

A whole lifetime of falling through the cracks down below, and it sort of pushes a body up here. Yeah, people used to say that here was for all people who couldn't survive down south. I don't think it's really that way. I think they just do things differently here. They don't want to be under anyone's thumb. Up here, you hoe your own row. You don't have to worry about what other people are doing and they don't bother with what you're doing.

Riches

I feel that I'm rich now. Money doesn't make you rich, it's how you feel. A person is only rich in proportion to the things he can do without, as far as I'm concerned. I'm not saying I wouldn't like a few dollars, but . . . I can't think of anything I'd want except a boat and a good motor.

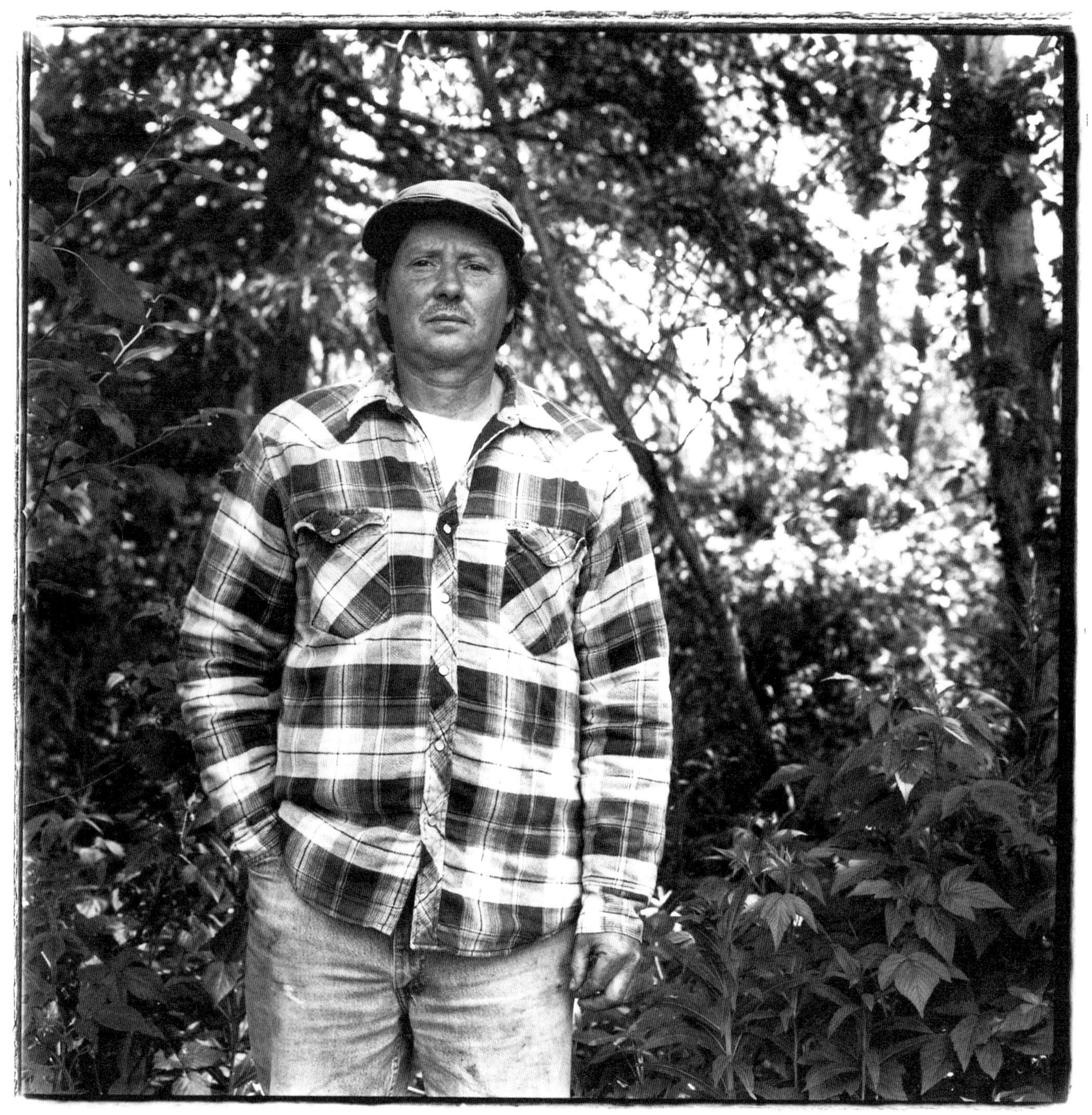

July 5

Sandra Hall
Dawson, YT

Born in 1955, Sandra was raised in Kelowna, British Columbia. After completing high school, she became an apprentice printer, then a house painter. She attended music school in Vancouver from 1986 to 1988. Sandra moved to the Yukon in 1989.

The green smell

When I got to Dawson, I knew within 24 hours that I was going to stay. I just knew it. It was the hottest day on record in May. The trees were doing their springtime burst and I got out of my van and filled my lungs with that green smell and that was it. I looked around and said, "Yeah, I like it here." There was a sense of recognition. Almost like I'd been looking for this place all my life. And when I found it—even though I wasn't aware I was looking for it—I knew. And I know that I'll be here until the day I die.

I've done three winters by myself—like living with myself. There are times that loneliness is palpable. You can see its shape. It comes in totally unexpectedly and lasts for about ten minutes and then it's gone.

The eye of the soap opera

Dawson, because it's such a small town, and because it is so isolated in the winter, you can't help but know everybody's business. And sometimes you don't want to. You don't want to be involved in the soaps. Like I was working at the Westminster Hotel and talk about a soap opera! That's the eye of the soap opera. Everything goes down there, you know. You miss 4 days and you miss 15 episodes.

The town's got to be OK. They let a convicted criminal be the mayor.

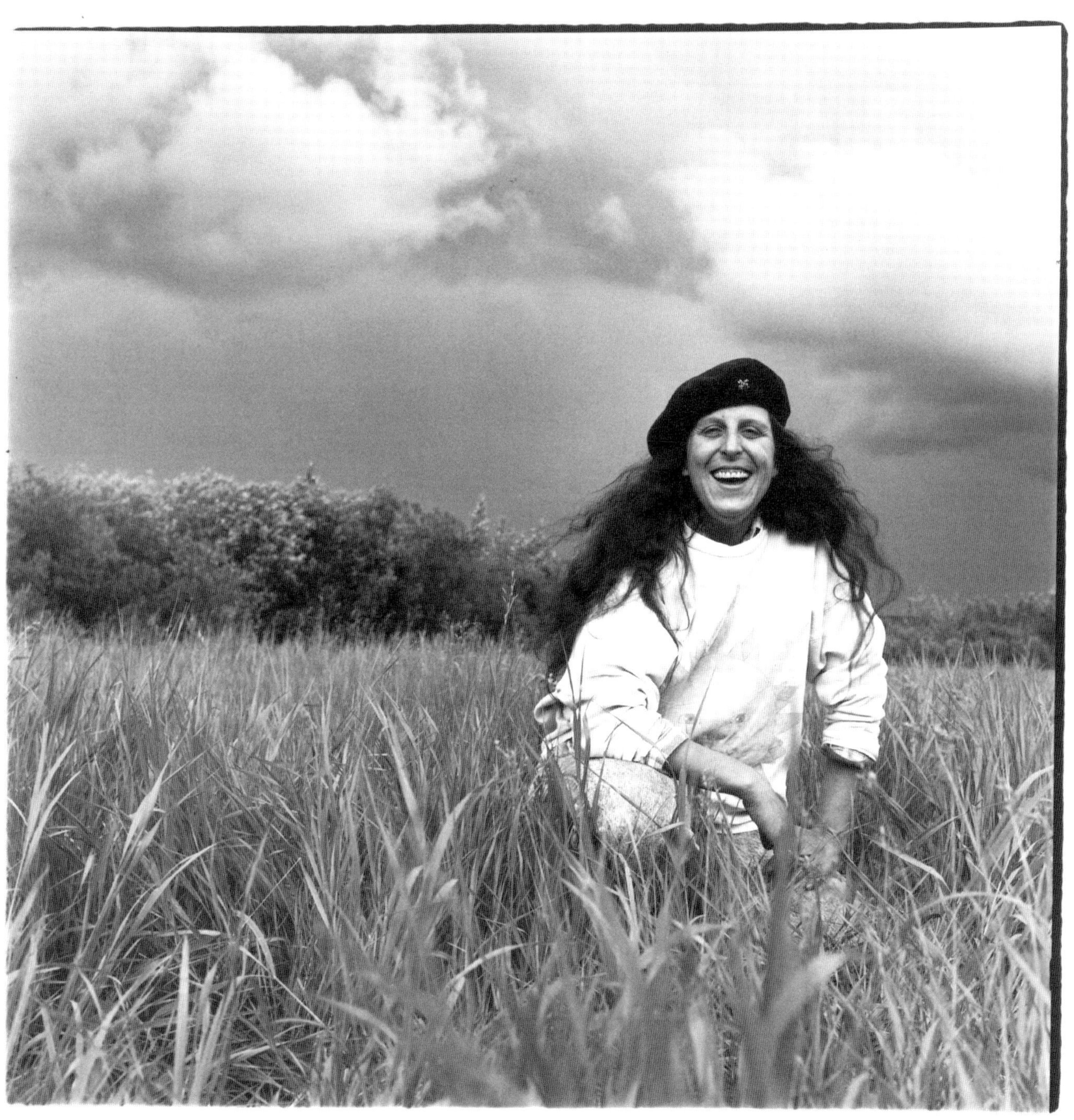

July 5

Jim Gaddie
Dawson, YT

Jim was born in 1947 in Sudbury, Ontario. After visiting the Yukon in 1972 and liking what he saw, Jim went home, loaded everything he owned onto a three-ton truck, and moved to the Yukon. Jim is a welder, gold miner, and truck driver.

The Yukon River

Too thick to drink, too thin to plow.

If he struck it rich

I think what I'd do is go mining until I was broke. Actually, I'd spend some of it on women, I'd spend some of it on whiskey, I'd gamble a little of it away, and the rest I'd just spend foolishly.

Dawson in the wintertime

The road comes in and stops. There's no through traffic. People don't come here to continue on. It's the end of the road and you're not at the end of the road by accident. You're at the end of the road because that's where you want to be.

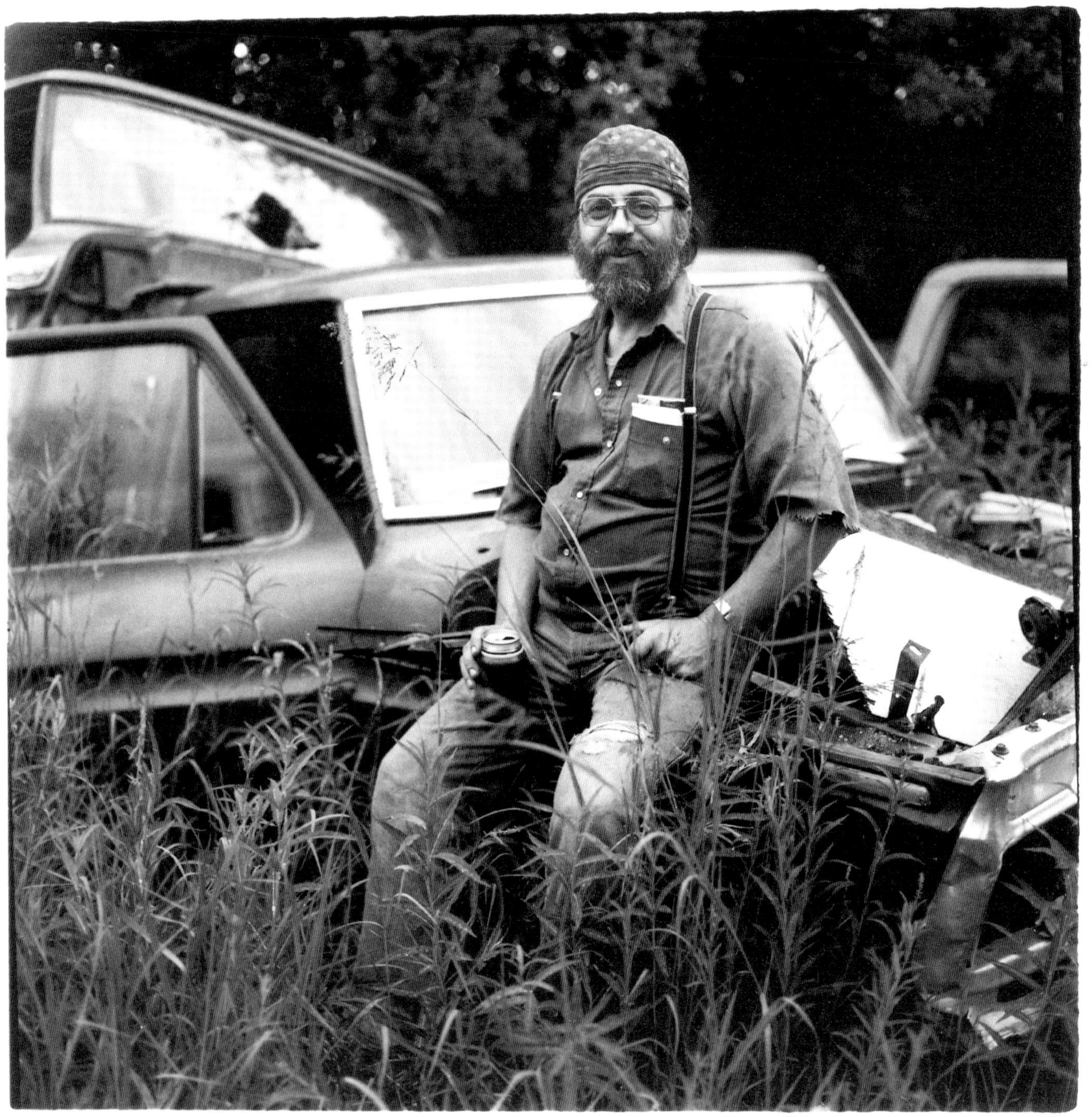

July 6

David Robinson
Dawson, YT

David was born in Hamilton, Ontario, in 1955. When he was 20, he hitchhiked to Dawson where he became a gold miner and a commercial fisherman. In 1987, he and a friend opened an outdoor supply store, The Dawson Trading Post. Dave works in the store eight months of the year. The rest of the year he spends on his trapline.

Paying for an apple from a poke of gold

When I was twelve years old, I saw this program on television. It was about this man. His name was Jeff Grand. He was from Alaska. It showed him trapping in the winter time. He was a guide in the summer. Every spring he would paddle his canoe 200 miles from his trapline to town. On his way down, he stopped at a trading post. He went in and took an apple off the counter. Then he took out a little poke of gold and a little pair of weigh scales, and he paid for the apple. To me, that was life.

Fitting into a puzzle

The first year I went trapping I was 26 years old. I felt like I could take on the world. I just wanted to go out and experience everything. The open wilderness. And things just came natural to me. It was like fitting into a puzzle. Talking to other people, I kind of feel that it was the same way with them too—that they went and kind of mixed in with the wilderness and things came natural. I've got no interest in ever going back down south again. No interest at all. This is what I want to do for the rest of my life. Without a doubt.

I've got two loves in my life. One is women and one is the bush. When I don't have one, I always have the other.

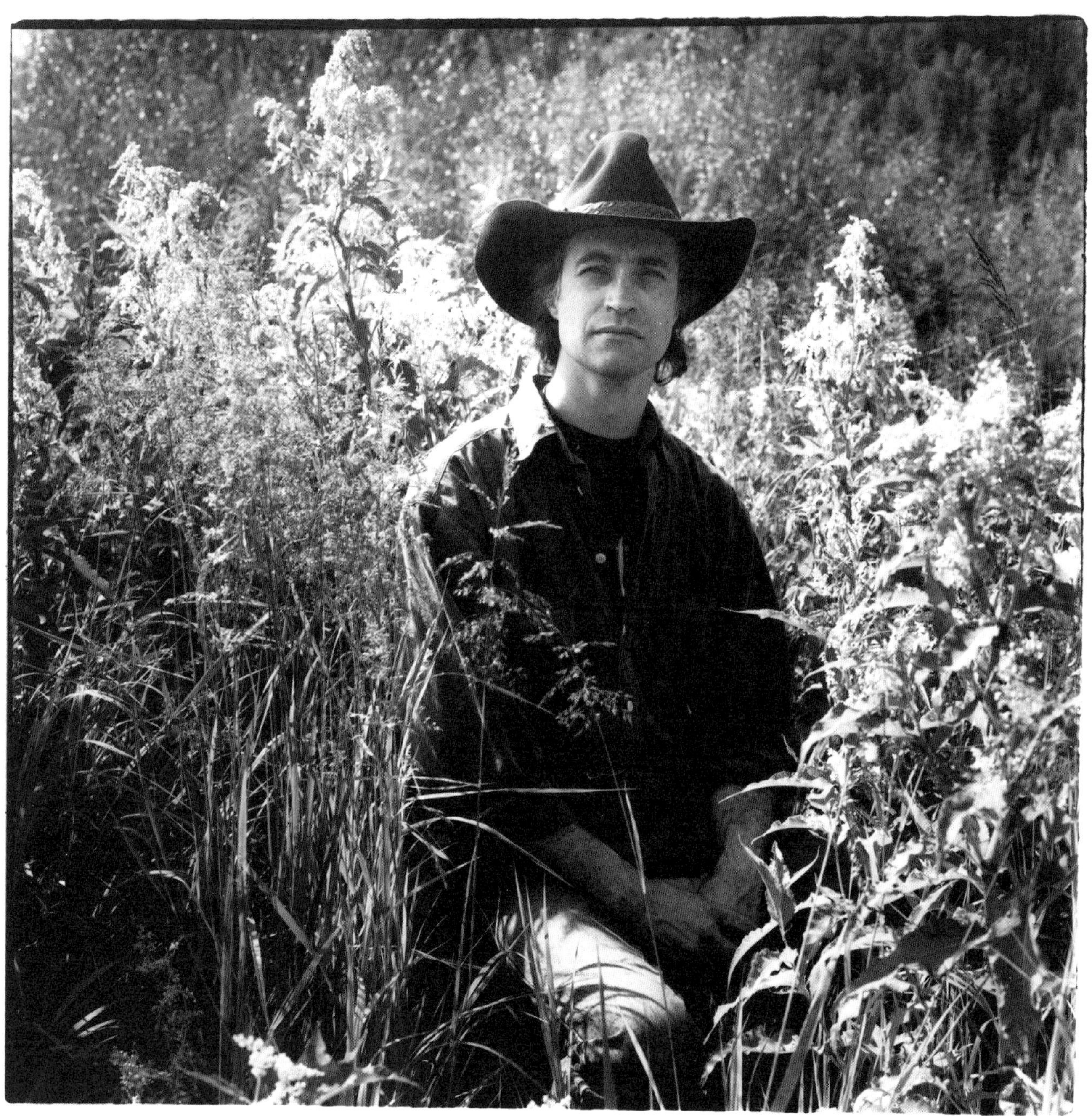

July 7

Bill Jackson
Dawson, YT

Bill was born in 1933 and grew up in Toronto. As a young man, he worked for Forestry in northern Ontario. It was there he developed a great love for remote places. Married in 1958, Bill and his wife had four children. He came to the Yukon in 1981. In 1984, Bill became the fire tower watchman in the Dawson area where he still works today.

The frog

They say that you can put a frog in hot water and he'll jump out, but if you put a frog in comfortable water and gradually heat it, you'll cook him to death. I have a feeling that's what it's like for people in the city.

That feeling

I love that feeling that there's real wilderness right at your back door. I can't live happily outside of that situation. I've tried cities, on and off. It just doesn't work. I like northern Ontario and I like the Rocky Mountains. I found the Yukon was a combination of both. I've always been interested in history and I've read a lot about the Klondike. Often while I'm up in the fire tower, I can actually look at the areas being mentioned in a book.

Bad bears

I'm getting to be a firm believer in log cabins out here with all the bears around. I find the strain of bear up here is quite aggressive compared to other places I've been.

The Yukon River

It's a fascinating river. It's a beautiful looking river. The sky above is always changing. I never get tired of looking at it.

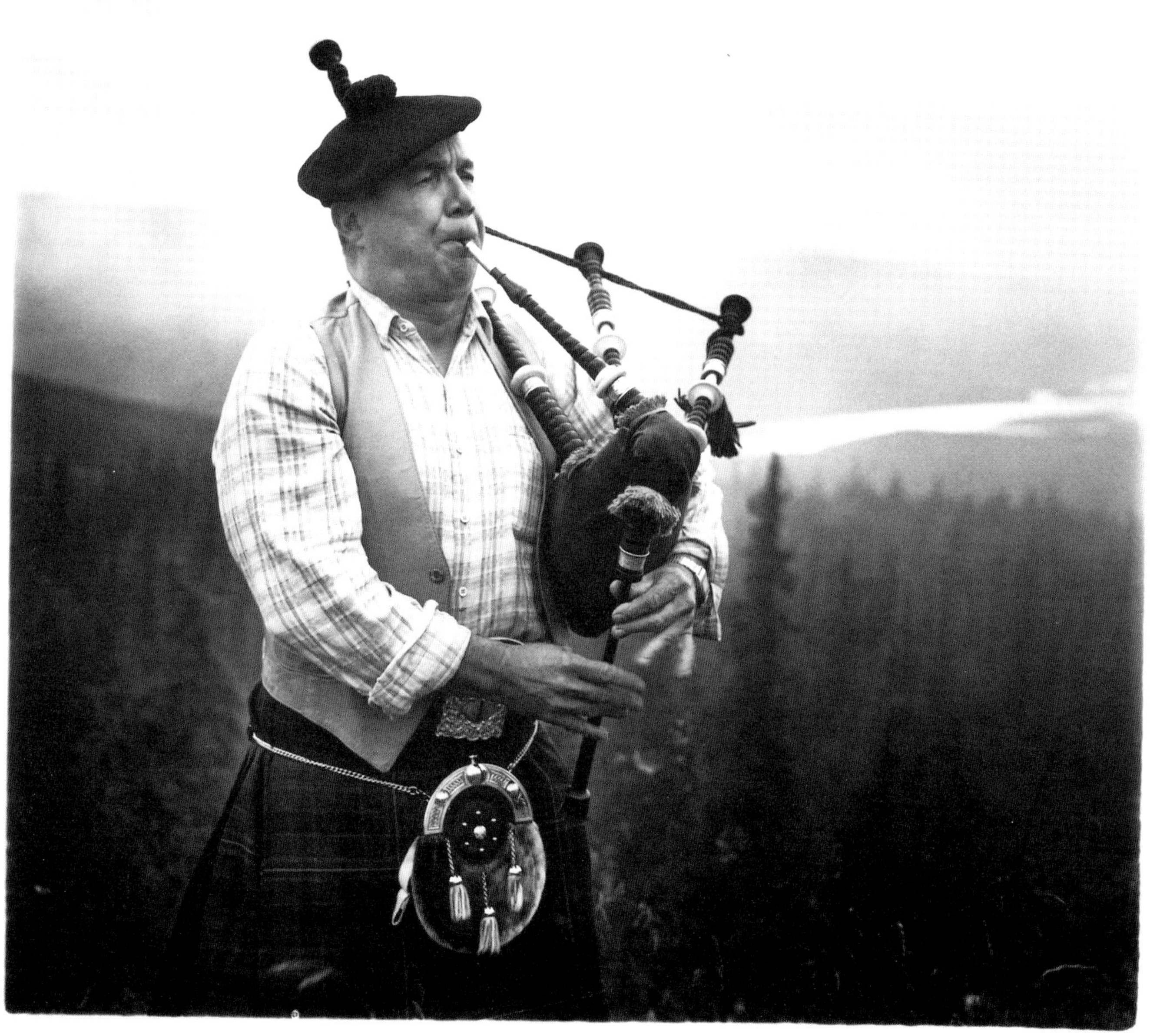

In 1927, Percy was born in the now abandoned village of Blackstone, Yukon Territory. In 1935, his family moved to Moosehide, a small Indian community near Dawson. Percy left school in grade three because his father needed help on the trapline. Besides trapping, he has been a deckhand on a freight boat, a sawmill operator, and a pilot on the Dawson ferry. Percy was chief of the Han Indian band from 1969 to 1983.

July 8

Percy Henry
Dawson, YT

The meeting

This is a story I got from an elder. It was about a hundred years ago. They called the chiefs from different places and they had a meeting. They talked about the river and they predicted the river would be polluted and the fish would be all gone. And now I see this happening. I see the fish going. One time, I could go out and set a net and catch fish and get enough for everybody to eat. Now you can't do that.

We have to work together or we're going to kill the land. Our elders told us not to point fingers at anybody because we have to work together, instead of me as an Indian and you as a white man.

They wait for jobs

They say, "Chief, what do you expect. Since I come out of school, I wait for a job and I'm still waiting. Promise, promise."

They say, "While I'm waiting, I have one beer. It's good. So I went to have another beer. Now I'm alcoholic."

Well, they're waiting for a job.

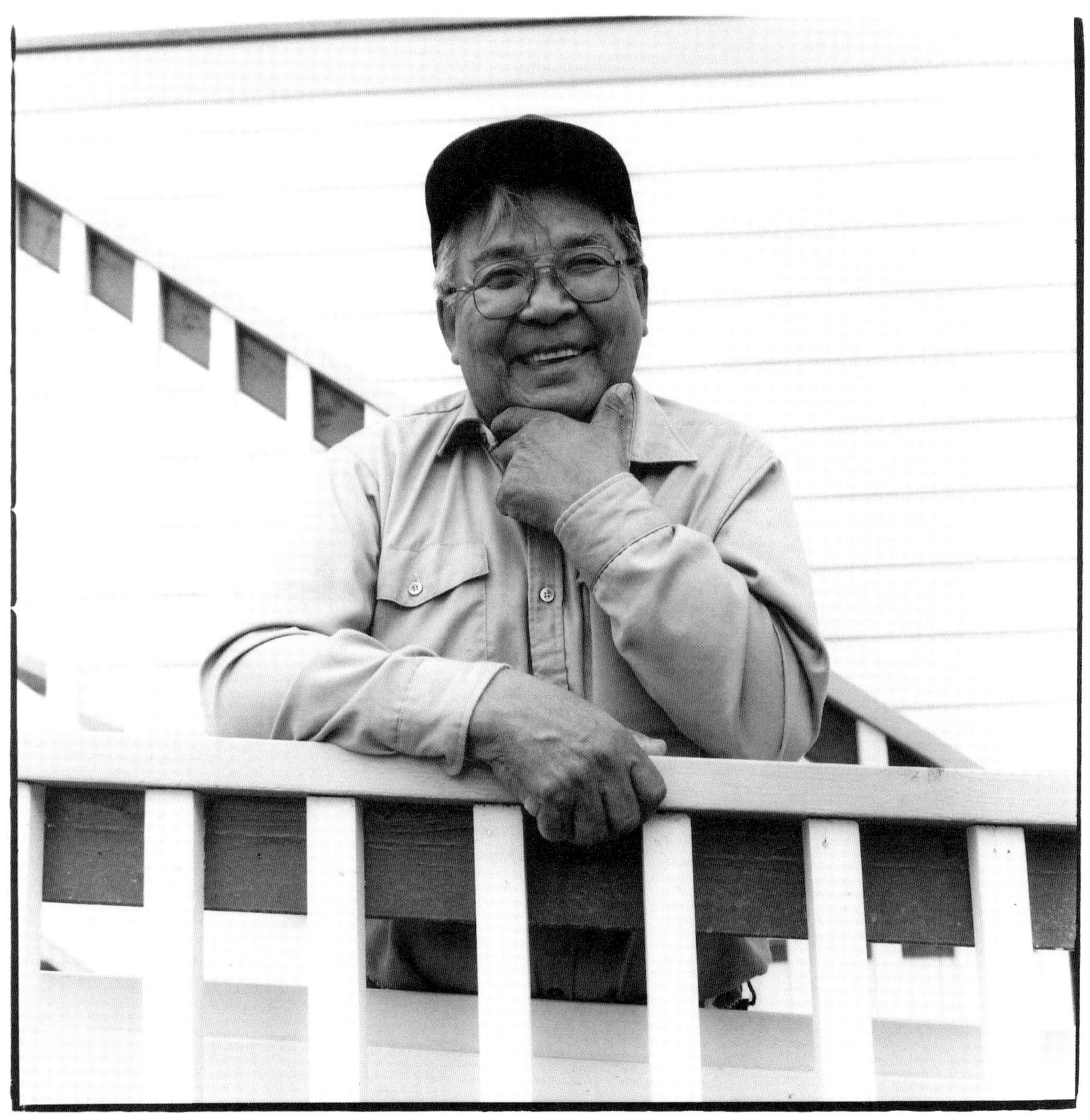

The daughter of a welder and now a housewife, Julie was born in Prince George, British Columbia, in 1966. She came to Whitehorse in 1992, but stayed for only two months because the city was "too busy" for her. When Julie met Cor Guimond in Dawson, he invited her to go commercial salmon fishing at his homestead, 35 miles downriver at Cassier Creek. Julie decided to stay permanently when she and Cor became romantically involved. Julie gave birth to their son Saidye in the spring of 1993.

July 10

Julie Hiller
Cassier Creek, YT

Red-necked people

What I am shocked at is, of the people I've met along the river, a lot of them just don't appreciate what they have here. To me, it just seems like we're lucky to be out here. Just to see it. It is just beautiful. But with other people—I don't know. They make it almost ugly with their attitudes. They don't appreciate the nature and what they've got. And they've chosen to live out here. I just meet so many bigoted, red-necked people on the river it just drives me crazy. See, I'm an open person. I don't care if they've got five legs or whatever.

The city, to me, in a range of colors, is more grayish. Whereas out here, it's so bright. Especially when the leaves come out. Wow, it's so nice. Or when it starts snowing. But in the city, you kind of miss all that.

Water

It was a kind of a thing for me. I wanted to get over my fear of water. Which I didn't really get over. You don't realize how dangerous it is. I always have visions of falling overboard when we're checking the nets. Getting caught in the net. It's calming to watch the river, though. It's just nice. It kind of flows by. You can almost put your problems in.

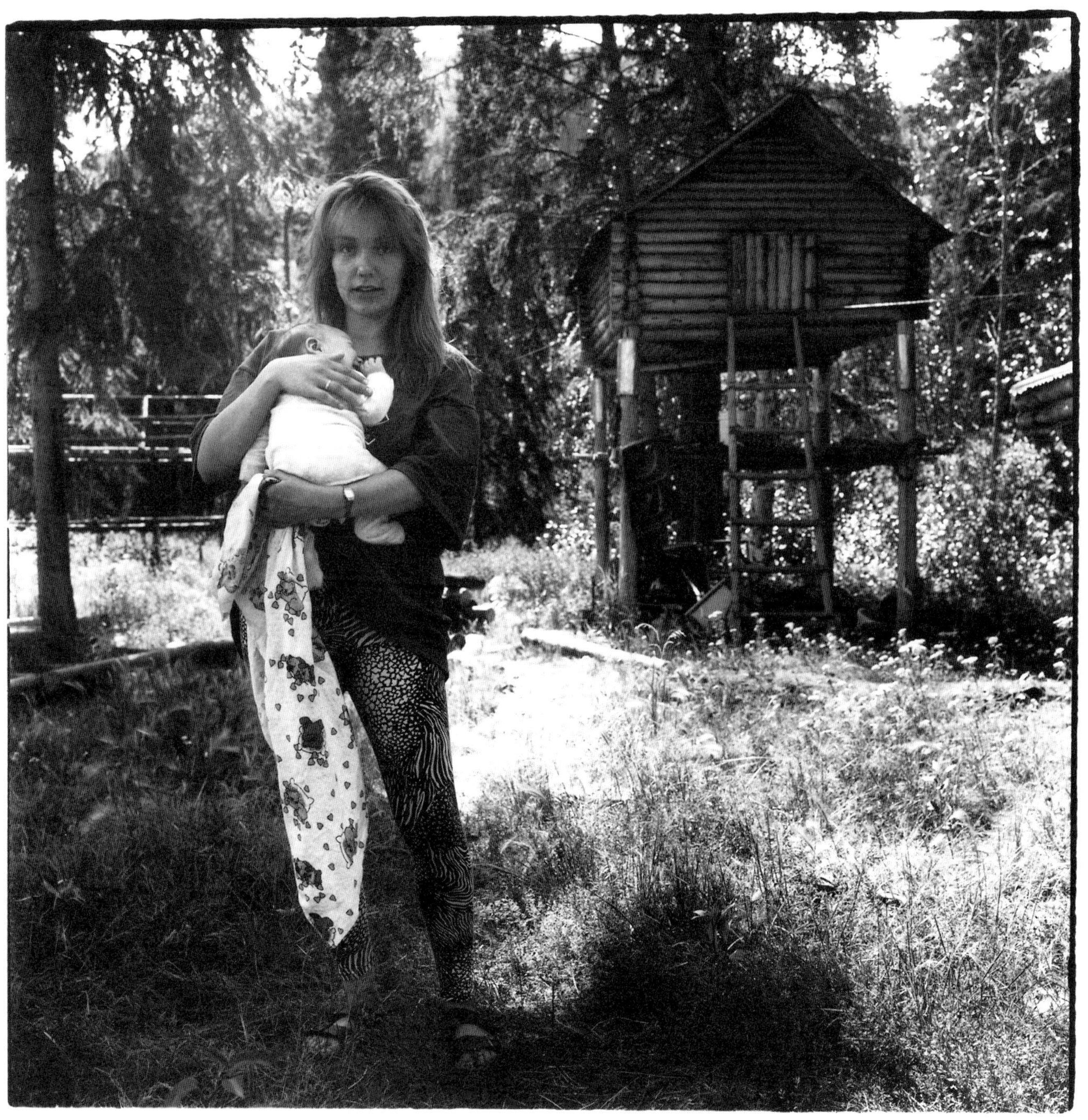

July 12

Shelly Brown
Sunset Creek, YT

Born in 1969, Shelly grew up in Fredericton, New Brunswick. She attended university for two years, then left school to work in a record store. At age 21, she moved to Jasper, Alberta. After staying a year and deciding the Rocky Mountains weren't wild enough, she headed for the Yukon. Shelly now lives in the bush 50 miles from Dawson with her boyfriend Sebastian. They fish commercially in the summers and mush dogs in the winters.

The nice hippie-looking guy

I didn't want to work in town. I wanted to go fishing. That's when I met Sebastian. I said, "I hear you're looking for someone to go fishing and I'd like to go."

Sebastian said, "OK, be here tomorrow at noon."

I liked him right away. His eyes were sparkling and he had this big smile on his face. I thought, "Right on! He's a nice hippie-looking guy. He's not a macho redneck." Zoom and away I went. I packed up everything.

But then I chickened out because my girlfriend said to me, "You're nuts! You don't even know this man and you're going to the bush to work with him alone? You're bonkers! Don't do it!"

So I went and told him I decided not to go, but he said, "Oh, come on. It'll be fun! I've got everything ready." He said, "Just try it for this week. If things don't work, that's no problem. You can come back."

So I said "OK."

Missing the land

When the summer ended, we decided to spend the winter together in Whitehorse. When we first came back to Dawson in the spring, I was walking along the river. Sebastian was walking ahead of me. I was crying, crying, crying.

He turned around, and when he saw me crying, he said, "I know."

He knew I was crying 'cause I missed the land so much. Something about this place that just gets in your soul.

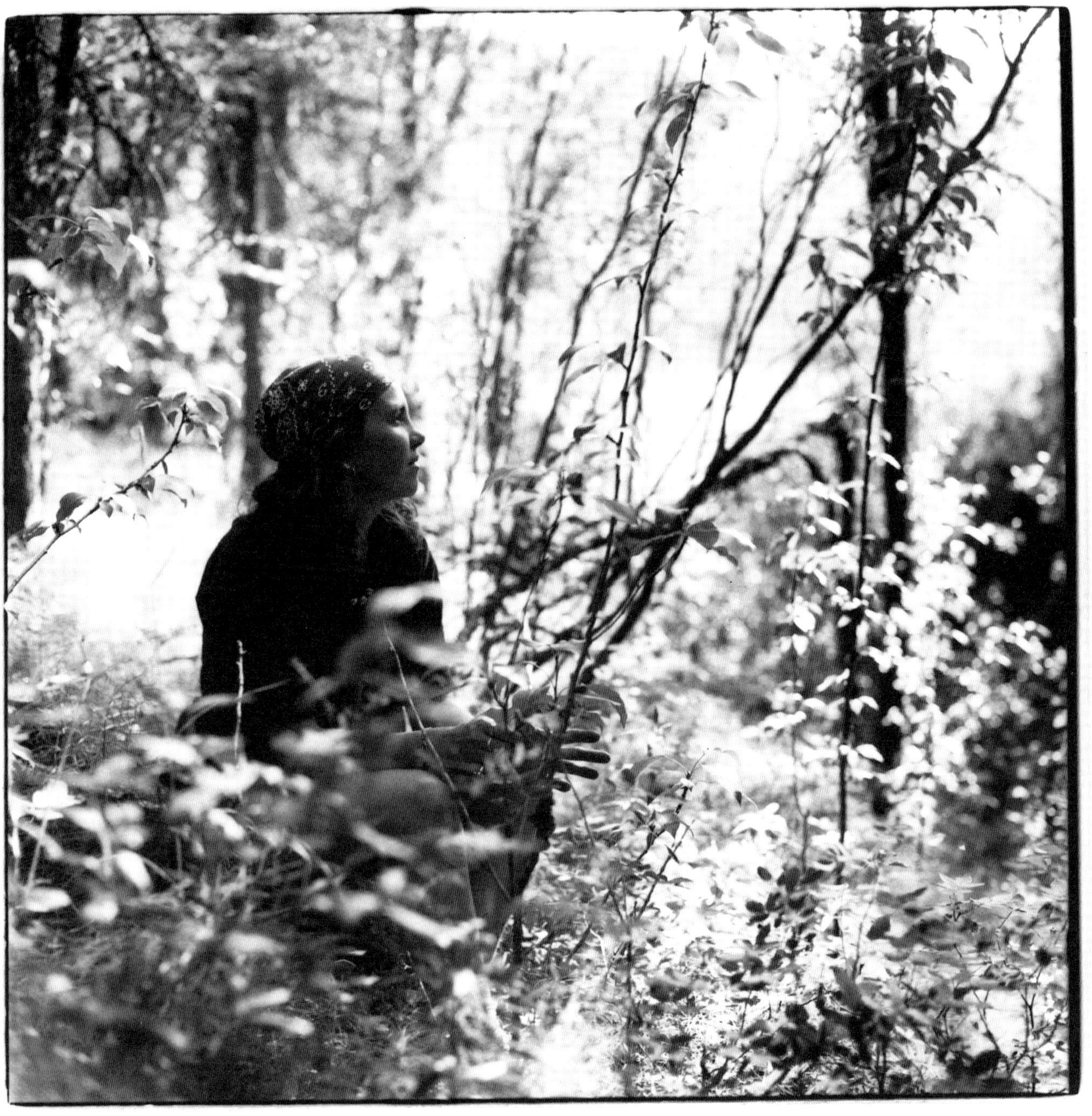

July 22

Bob and Mary Petersmark
Circle, AK

Bob and Mary drove to Alaska from Mississippi to visit their daughter who lives in Fairbanks. While in Alaska, they decided to explore the state in their camper. Bob is a recently retired postal worker and Mary is a housewife.

Alaskans

Bob: You can't tell people by the clothes they're wearing. You could be looking at a millionaire and they'd be dressed up just like a lumberjack.
Mary: They do love flowers. They just love flowers.
Bob: . . . and they're extremely friendly, the people up here. Much more friendly than our area. We were sitting here last night and this native fellow walked over and gave us some frozen king salmon. How many people are going to walk up and give you some sockeye for lunch, you know? But they do it up here.
Mary: . . . and they're not suspicious up here. They're much more trusting.
Bob: I see a spirit up here that's kind of a rebel. I notice it because I've got a smidgen of that in me too.

Driving to Alaska

Bob: We drove 4,113 miles in four days. We moved right along and didn't do a whole lot of sleeping.

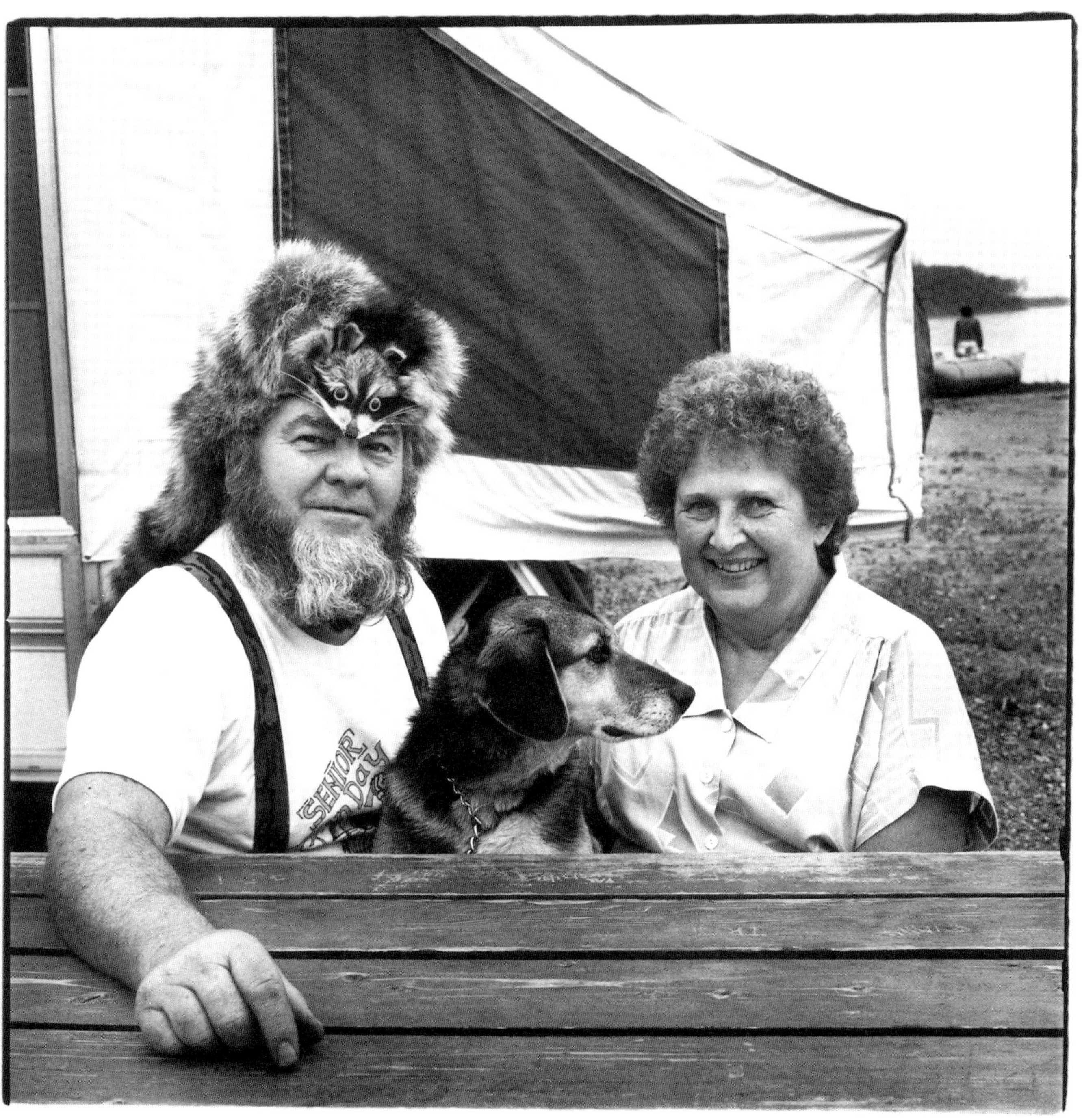
SENIOR
Day

July 22

Ed Moore
Circle, AK

Being mysteriously vague, Ed told us he was born on the east coast of the United States in the early 1930s and that he joined the U.S. Air Force in 1950. It was with the service that he first came to Alaska. He has been a miner, carpenter, farm hand, railway laborer, and fisherman.

Harmony

I was looking for this place right here. I was always looking for it. Look at this beautiful scenery. How can you beat this? It's hypnotic, it really is. You can see moose walking around and the bear and the geese and the ducks. The river flowing. It's full of salmon. You see harmony. Everything is flowing together, it's not pulling apart. It's so peaceful.

Down below, in the lower 48, I ran hard. I always ran hard. I worked sometimes 15, 18, 20 hours a day. For what? Building empires that really mean nothing. Now this here, I could not buy. All the money I earned in my entire life and I couldn't buy this. This is free. It's beautiful, it really is.

As far as you can see

There's not one telephone pole, not one wire, not one flag pole or antenna . . . not one light at night . . . nothing as far as the eye can see.

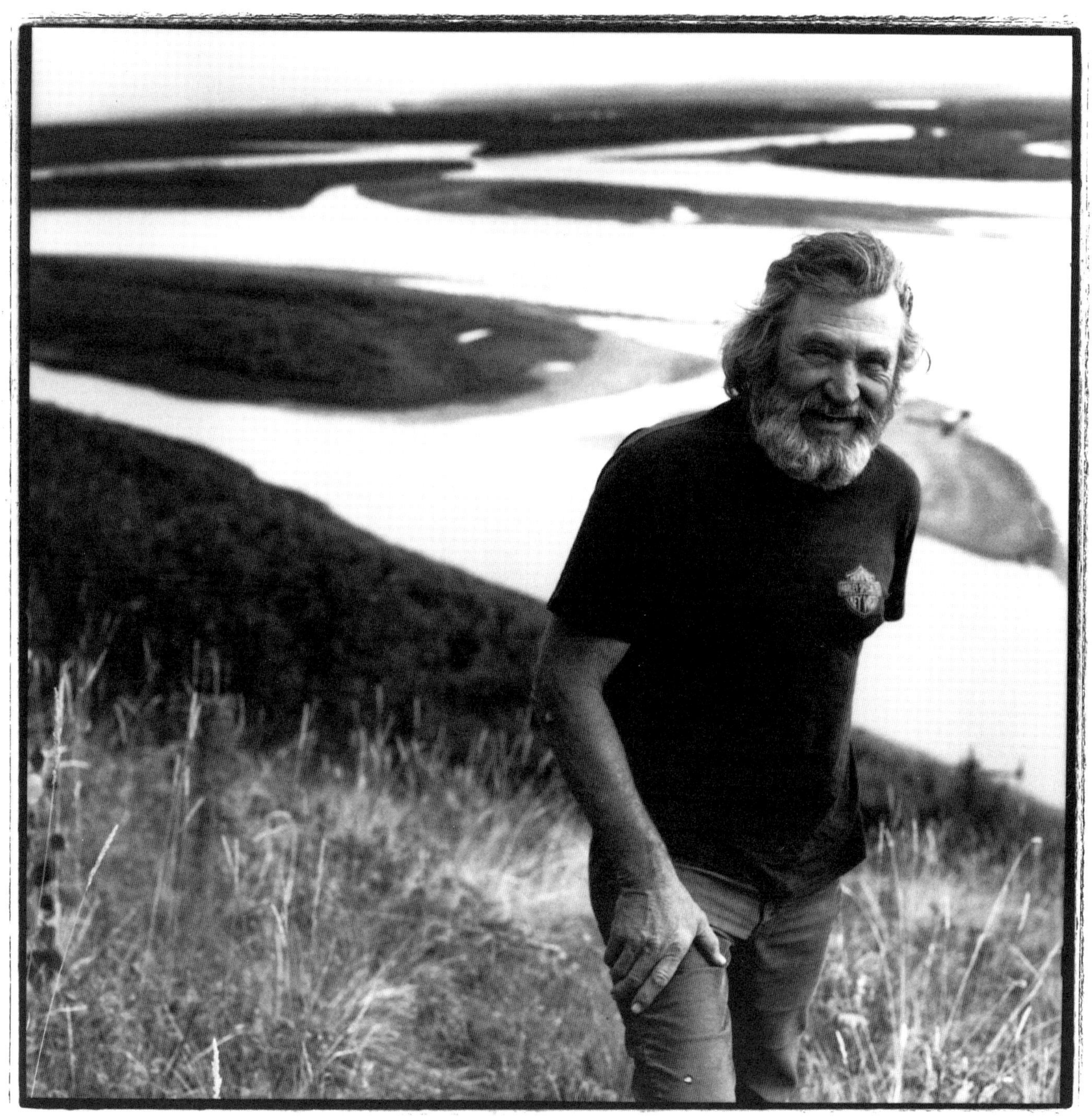

July 22

Larry Nolan
Albert's Fish Camp, AK

Larry was born in 1961, in Erwin, Tennessee. After graduating from high school in 1980, he began working for the U.S. Forest Service. He is presently the crew boss of a fire fighting crew in Alaska.

One trip and one look

I love it here. The wide open spaces. Not a lot of people. No hustle and bustle. It just seems like since I was little, Alaska was always a part of me. I took one trip and one look and it's like I'm supposed to be here.

My grandmother

My mother was always sick when I was younger. My grandmother raised me—she's my best friend, my brother, my sister, my mom, my dad. I can't just abandon her. It hurts her when I leave for six or seven months of the year. But she knows I love the job.

Donna

I lost a girlfriend in a car accident about three weeks before I came out this year. She was going to come up and spend the summer. She's got a birthday this month. She would be 28. This morning, I thought a lot about her. After seeing her for 12 years, I thought about not coming back, but she would have said, "You know how much you love your job, and you love Alaska."

This morning I got to the edge of the river and just sat down and watched the smoke, inversion, and fog. You feel how small you are compared to the river and this land. Really brings out things in your heart, in your soul.

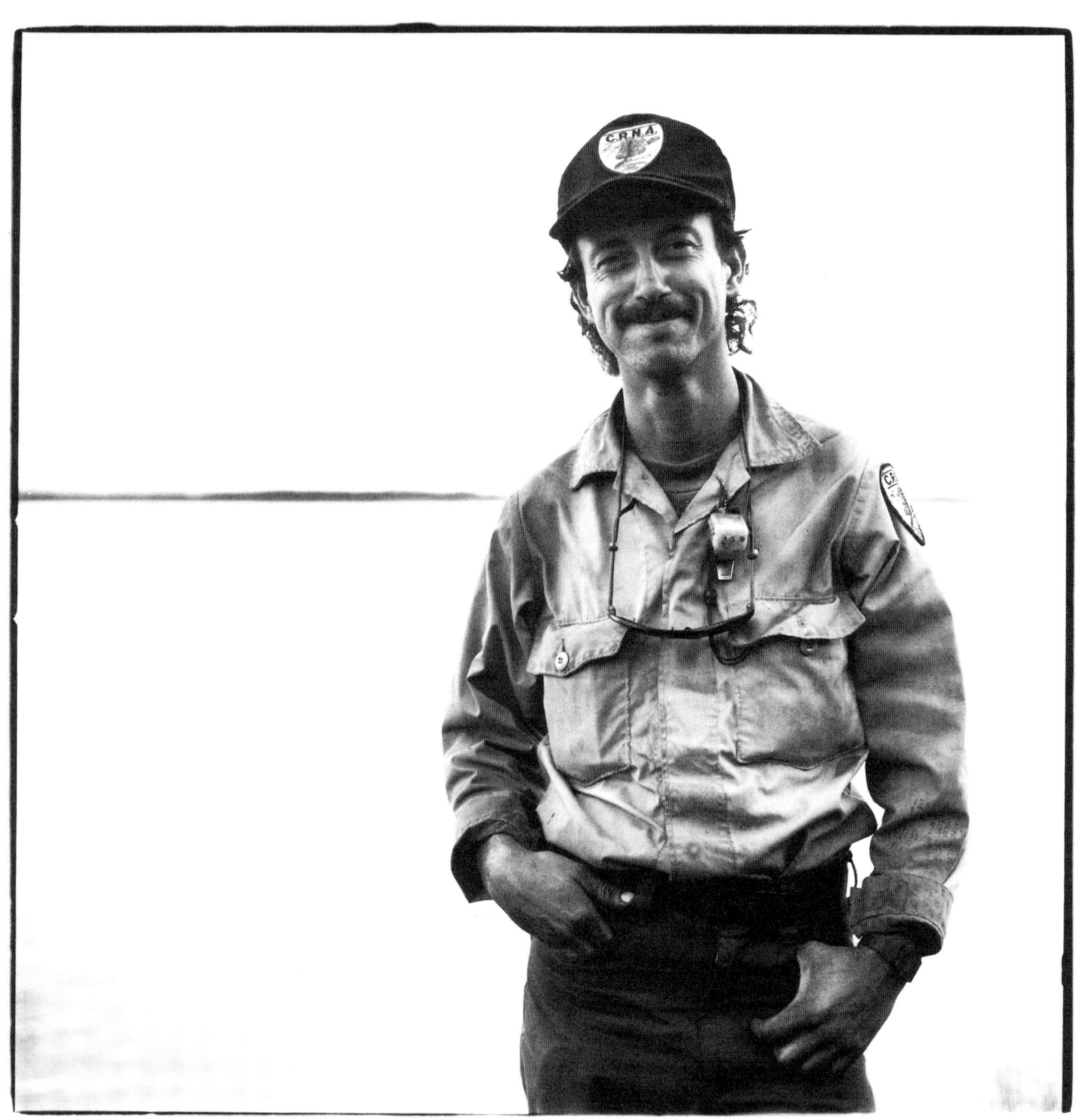
C.R.N.A.

July 27

Dave Stewart
Fort Yukon, AK

Dave was born in 1961 in Roseburg, Oregon. He first was introduced to the wilderness at age 10, when his family moved to Glide, Oregon. Married at 19, his first son was born while Dave was running from the law in Alaska. He turned himself in at age 22, and spent a year in jail during which time his second son was born. When his marriage ended a few years ago, Dave was awarded custody of his children. Presently, Dave and his two sons live in Fort Yukon where he helps his aunt and uncle manage the Sourdough Hotel.

Living in the right time

Before I moved here, I always thought I was a person that should have been born a hundred years earlier—back when the Indians were still there and the hunting was really good. When I moved here it was like I moved into the time I was suppose to live in.

When I go out hunting, I'm out there, hundreds of miles from anyone—any town—anywhere. You don't have to worry about someone breathing down your neck all the time. I found it was getting like that in Oregon. Places where I used to catch steelhead? Now people are just lined up. People used to grow pot up in the mountains too, and it brought the police. You couldn't even go deer hunting without airplanes bombing around wondering what you were doing. Moving here, I see caribou by the thousands. Two whole days they were going across the Porcupine River. Every second of two full days there was caribou in the water.

Someday I hope I can find someone that I can share all that with, you know, someone that likes to do that kind of stuff.

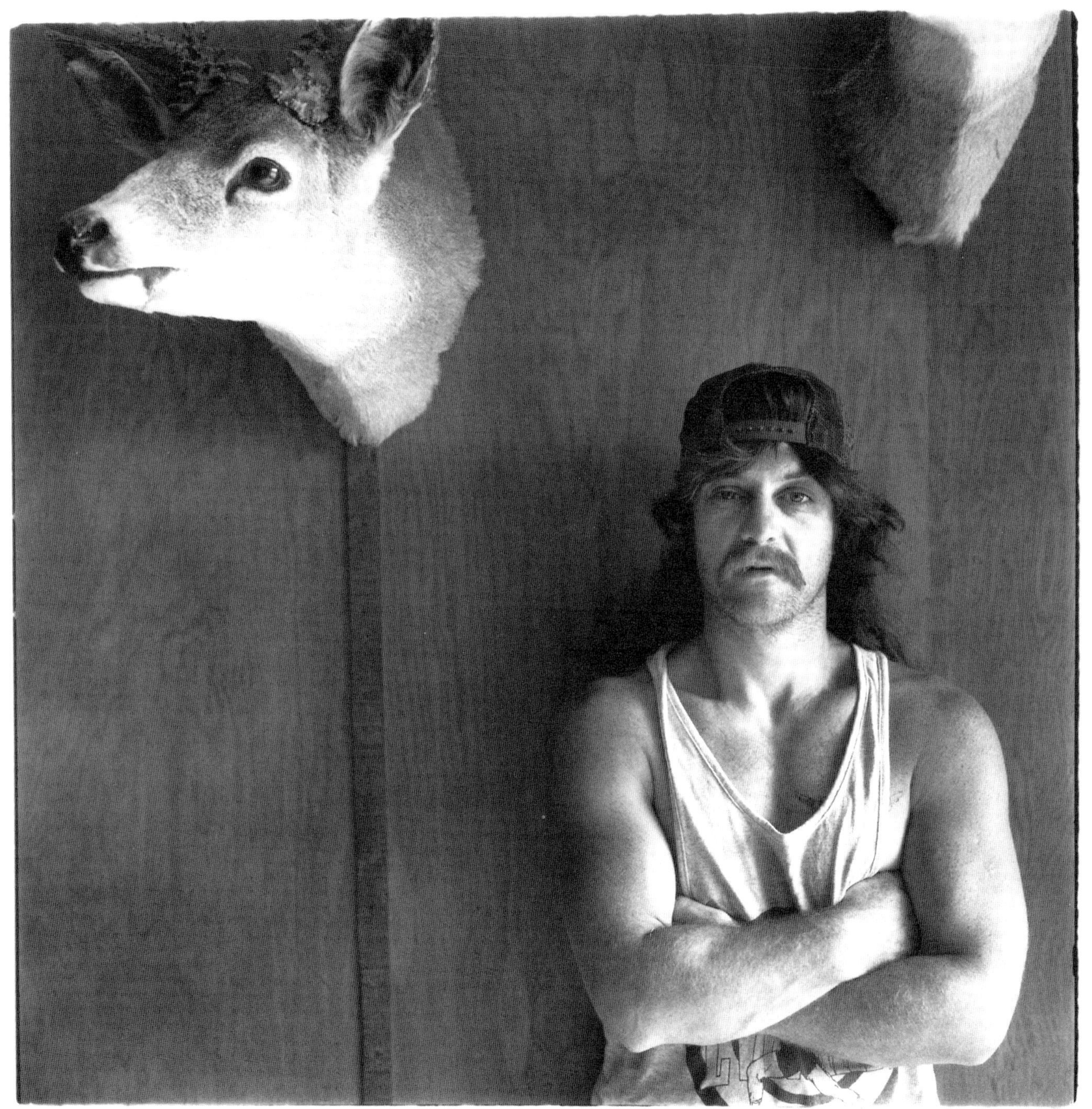

July 28

Heimo Korth
Fort Yukon, AK

Heimo was born in Germany, 1955, and his family moved to Wisconsin when he was a small boy. In 1974 he took a summer job as a hunting guide in Alaska's Brooks Range. He liked Alaska so much he decided to make it his home. Heimo met his wife Edna on St. Lawrence Island in the Bering Sea. They have two children; a third daughter, Coleen, was lost in the Coleen river of northeast Alaska.

The nightmare

When I got there, to the Brooks Range, I said to myself, "I'm going to live here." The mountains, sheep all over, caribou, moose, bears, you know. That's what I wanted.

I said, "I'm not going to leave. In fact I'm gonna die out here."

I was so terrified of leaving that I was having nightmares. I knew this was home. It was just a weird feeling. I was almost in tears. I can't leave this place. No I can't do it. It was so strong. It was so strong.

Coffee, tea, juice, water, or wife

The first time I ever saw Edna was in her uncle's house. She came in and visited for awhile. She kinda looked at me, but she didn't pay any attention to me. Just another white guy. And so then she went out.

All of a sudden her uncle said, "That's Edna Rose. You should marry her."

Then one day her dad saw me and he said, "You come over. Come over and visit us."

I says, "All right."

So my friend Phil and I went over. We sat down at the table and her dad says to Phil, "What do you want, coffee or tea?"

He says, "Tea."

So then he asks me, "You want coffee, tea, juice, water, or wife?"

He was joking, but I ended up marrying her anyways.

Two wings

I've got to have both. I got to have Edna and that way of life up there on the Coleen River. I'm like a bird, you see. She's like one wing and the land is like another wing. If you take one away, I'll fall down, you see. You understand? I've got to have them both.

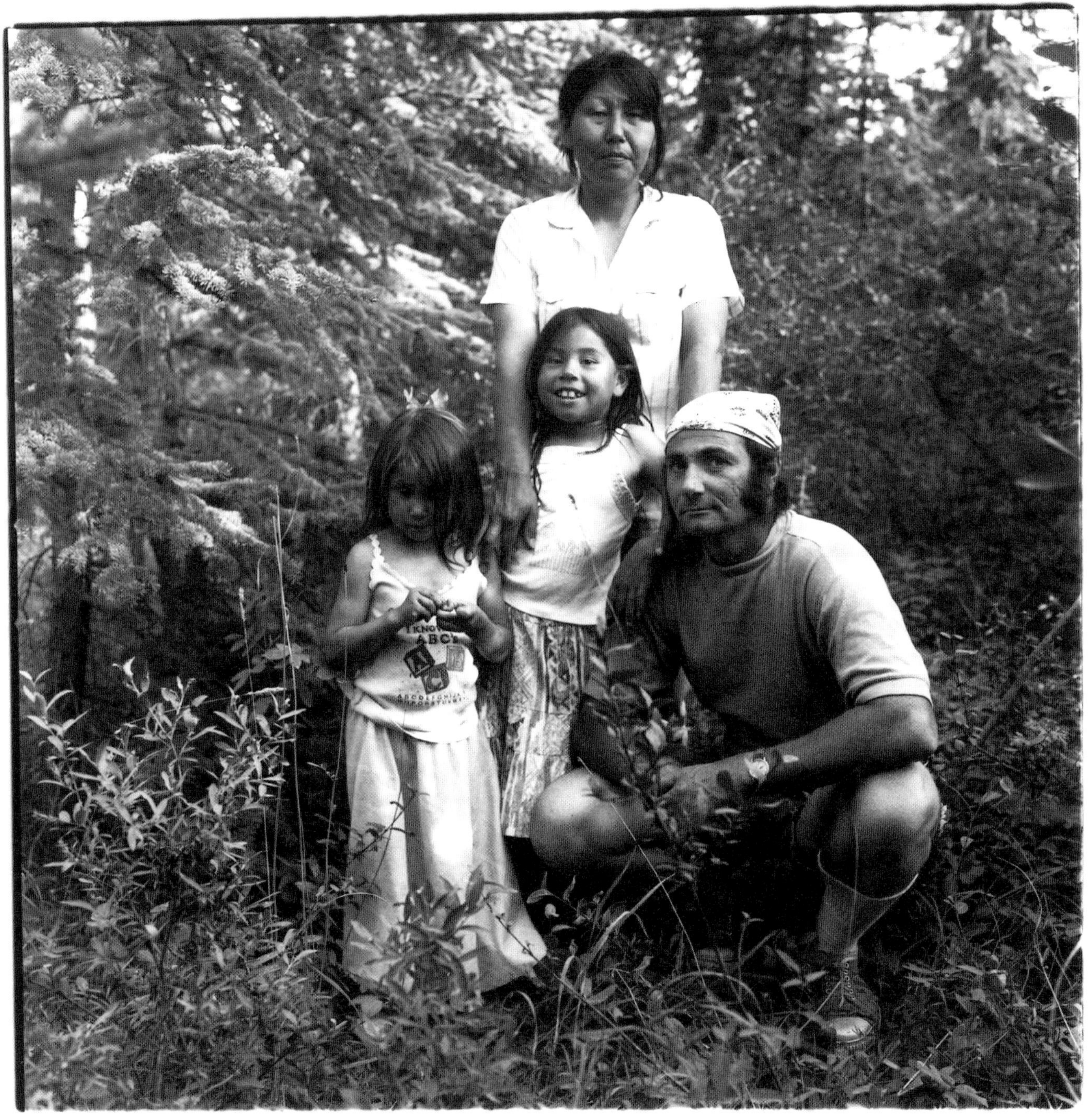

August 1

Florida Gieike
Beaver, AK

Florida was born in a fish camp along the Yukon River. She married as a young girl and had 14 children as well as adopting 5 others. Florida has worked as a day care worker and a cultural heritage instructor in the Anchorage school district.

What dividing the land did

In the early days people just wandered around and this whole land was their land. There were no boundaries. People were just free to come and go if they wanted to. We were free. Like an animal is free to roam around out there. And after they divided the land, like this is Federal land and this is State land, I think it really did something to our native people.

In the old days when we were in fish camp, if the water was low, and the fishing was bad, my dad would move the fish wheel. He'd see how good that new spot was. If that was no good, he would move it again someplace else. Sometimes he would move it just a couple of yards and it would be a better spot. You can't do that now.

Grammas (grandmothers)

We had all kinds of grammas. Even though they weren't related to us we would still call them grammas. They were such wonderful old people. All these grammas had their nets in the eddy in front of town. They'd go down there and cut their fish. I just loved to eat raw fish eggs. Those grammas would find fish eggs—good looking raw fish eggs—and they'd call me, wherever I was. I would run down there and I would eat my delicious red fish eggs. That's how kind they were.

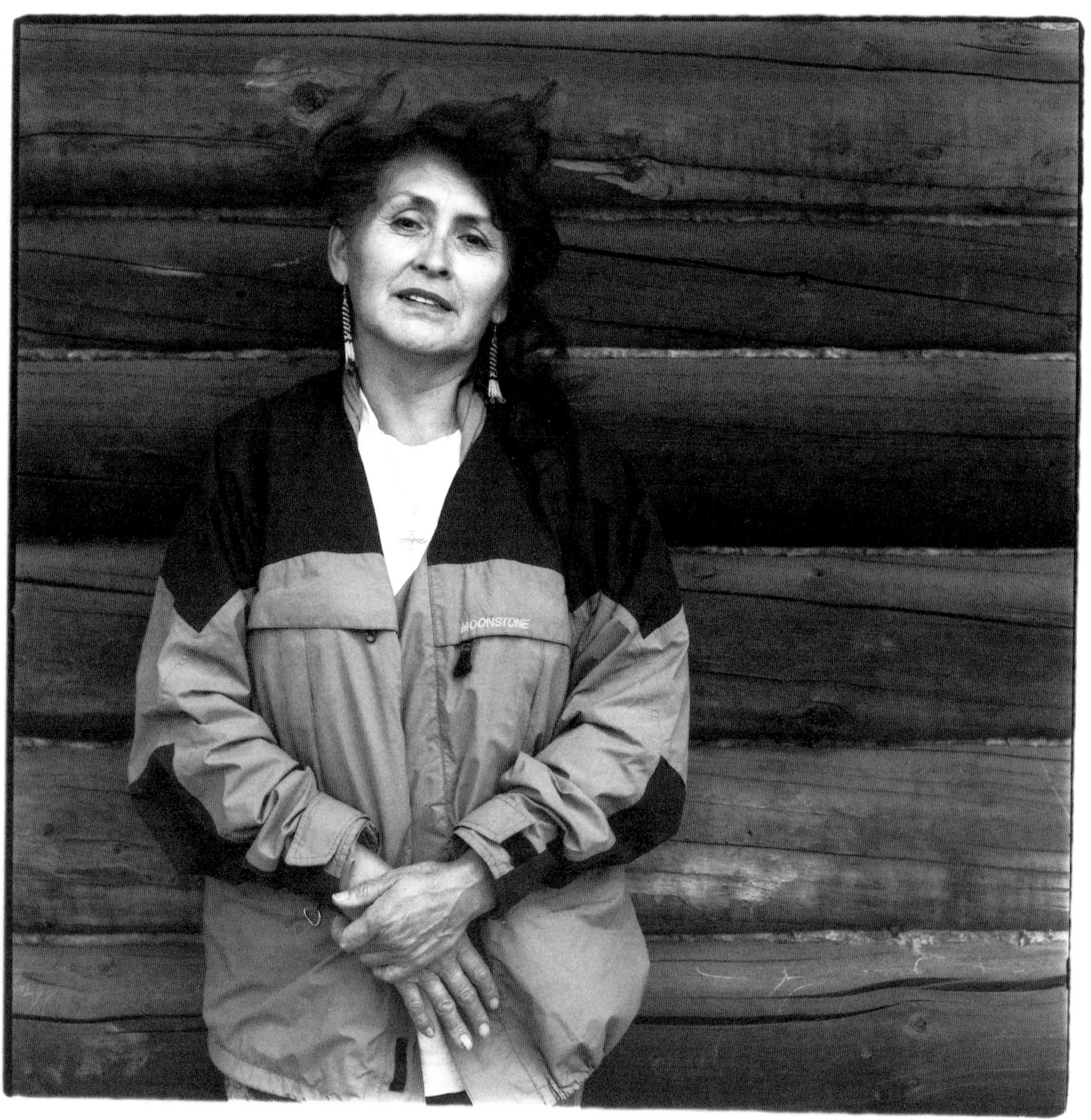
MOONSTONE

August 3

Peter Kokes
Beaver, AK

Peter was born in Chicago, Illinois, in 1938. After finishing college in 1960, he and his wife moved to Alaska. The couple taught in Nome, Alaska, for several years before returning to Wisconsin. While his wife raised their five children, Peter was a high school principal, a tavern owner, and a self-employed businessman. After the breakup of their marriage, Peter returned to Alaska. He moved to Beaver when he found a teaching position there.

The limelight

It's strange when you get off the plane in Beaver. When the plane flies over, all the snow machines go out to the airport to see who's getting off the plane. The whole village comes out. They meet every plane. You get off the plane, and you really feel like you're on display. Nobody's talking. Everybody's standing there, watching. Even today, when I fly into Beaver, it's a funny feeling. I don't like to be in the limelight.

I think a lot of people who are here have gone through a lot of things before they came here. I think many people who are here are scarred by something. Maybe that's why they've come here. And I don't mean running away from something. They've had life experiences that have disillusioned them somehow.

Leaving Wisconsin

We decided to get married on Wednesday, got married on Saturday, and left for Alaska. We drove across the country in a 1956 Ford; it was 1960. Took us three weeks. I was impressed. I'd never seen mountains before. I'd never been out of Wisconsin.

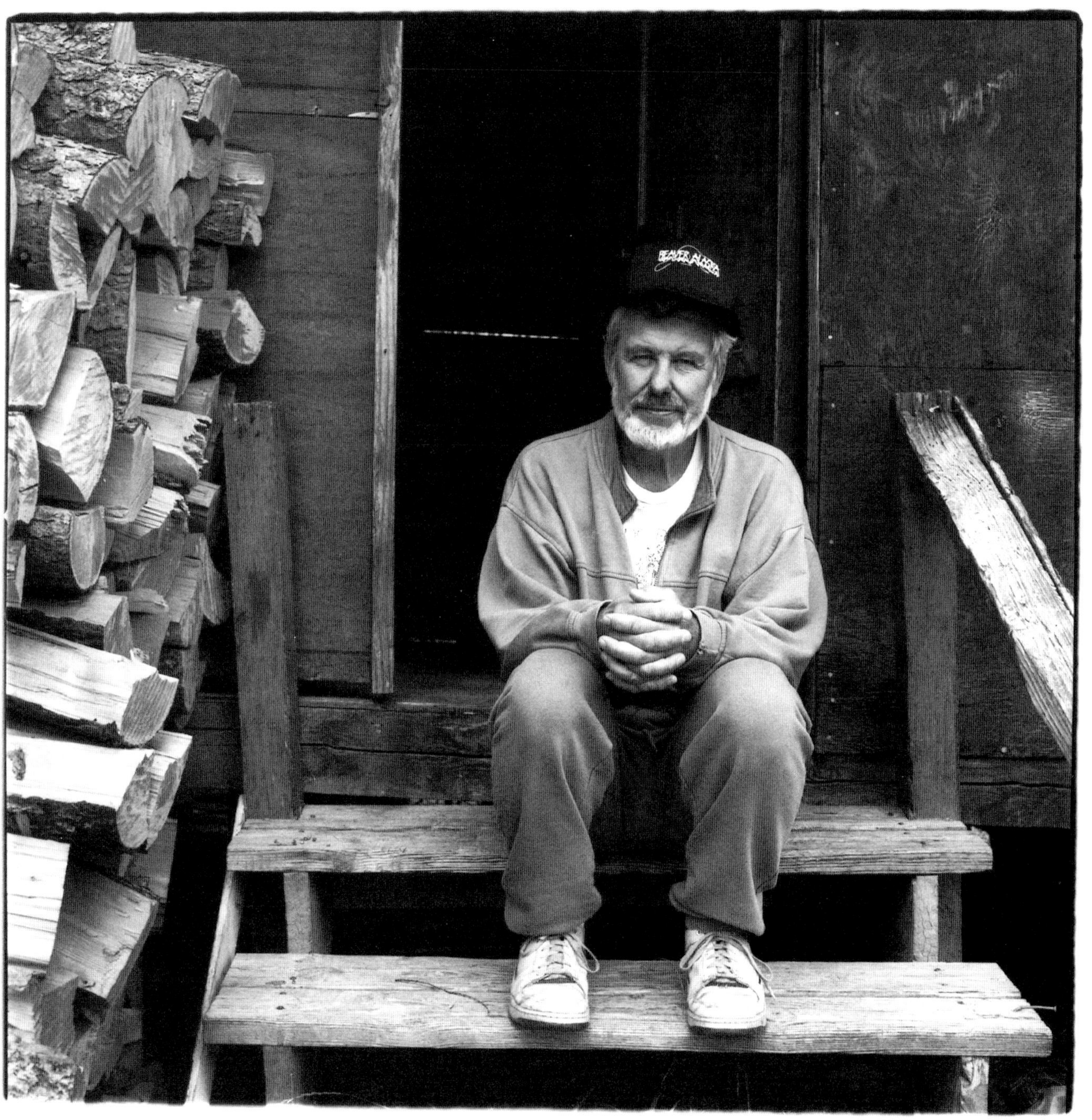
BEAVER ALASKA

August 10

Kitty Evans
Rampart, AK

Kitty was born in Rampart, Alaska, in 1914. She was married in 1932 to a trapper and fisherman. They had nine children. A widow now, Kitty is a well loved and respected elder in her community.

Progress

On our boat we didn't have an engine, no kicker, nothing. Just poling boats. We'd pole up the river. Sometimes we hitched one dog to the boat and he pulled us up. We used to pole up from way down the river. With a stick. That's what we used to do a long time ago. Nowadays, they got these fast boats, you can't see anything. Can't see moose or bear. Go real fast.

Don't come back

I had so many kids, we were always broke. My daughter put herself through school. She went to school in Fairbanks, finished, and then went to school out in the states. During the summer, she was an airline stewardess, and put herself through college. Now she's in Juneau, teaching. I told my kids to just not come back, because there'd be nothing for them here to do. They come back and visit.

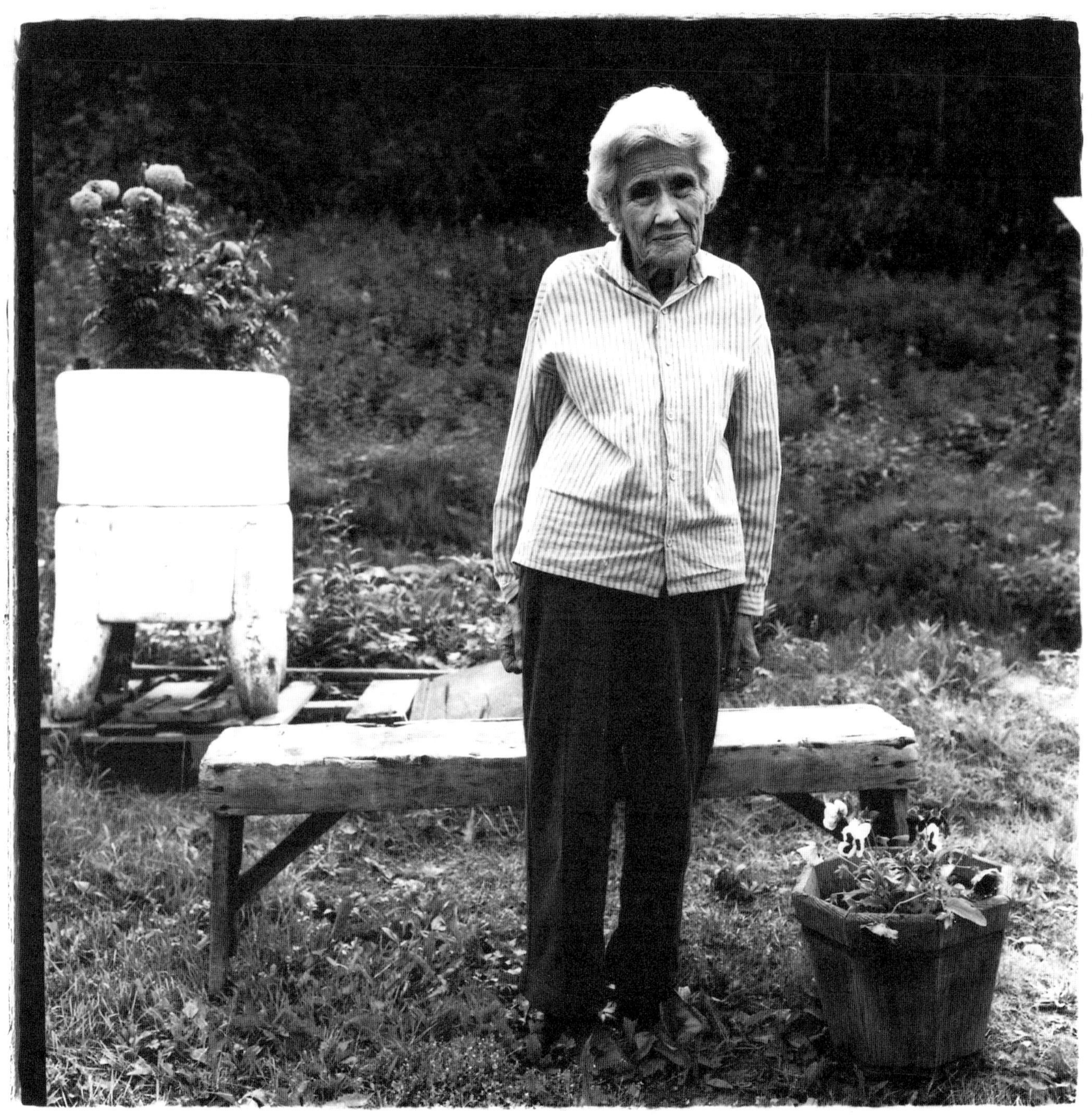

Rampart to John's Homestead, Alaska

"My Heart" Milepost 1,150, Tanana • *The Potlatch*

After pouring all day, it is still raining when we stop for the night a few miles before Rampart. Then, as we make camp, the rain stops and the sky turns a warm pink. Shafts of sunlight strike the distant islands. Across the river, mist on the mountains drifts away as geese fly overhead. Kathleen spreads a multicolored assortment of wet clothing over a clump of brilliant yellow willows to dry, then we sit companionably on a driftwood log eating grilled cheese sandwiches and drinking whiskey-spiked coffee.

The rain starts again halfway through supper, at first softly, then in a sudden torrent. We throw everything under the canoe and run for the tent.

"I wonder if we'll ever finish this trip," I say, curling tightly into my sleeping bag.

"Probably not," Kathleen predicts, folding her sweater into a pillow. "I bet we fall in love with a couple of trappers and never leave Alaska."

We meet Martin Bradley at the laundromat in Rampart a few days later. A grin splits his pale, freckled face when we tell him about our project. "I know just who you should interview," he says. When the laundry is done, we walk to the edge of town, then follow a narrow path through the trees.

"We're almost there," says Martin a few minutes later, smoothing his shirt and raking an impatient hand through his unruly hair. When we see a large cabin through the trees, Martin calls out, "Hey, mum—I brought some girls to see you!"

Kitty Evans is in her garden, pulling weeds from a patch of marigolds that grow from the top of an old washing machine. With some trepidation, the elderly native woman agrees to the interview, but smiles sweetly when we leave to fetch the camera and tape recorder.

After the interview, Martin invites us to a funeral potlatch the next day in Tanana. Because it is too far to arrive in time by canoe, he arranges for us to go with him and his friends in their boat.

We push off the next day, after loading our canoe and gear into the long, flat-bottomed riverboat. Rampart isn't even out of sight when Martin goes to the bow with a fiddle and a bottle of whiskey. Facing us, he starts to play a lively jig, taking occasional nips from a whiskey bottle tucked between his feet. While the others sing along in enthusiastic, discordant harmony, I lie on my back and watch the clouds whiz by with dizzying speed. It is marvelous not to be paddling.

It is almost dark when Martin and others begin singing a rhythmic Indian song. The song, full of longing and urgency, drifts across the black water.

"That's Tanana over there," says Martin, pointing to a small cluster of buildings on the riverbank. "In the old days, people used to sing this song when they came to a village."

In the distance, dark shapes run to the riverbank, and they too begin to sing. Someone shoots a gun into the air, then a chorus of dogs begins to howl.

"Now there's a proper welcome!" says Martin, jumping ashore with the bowline.

Like most villages along the river, Tanana consists of a few roads running parallel to the river. Boats and dogs line the riverbank, and, behind that, there is a church, nursing station, school, post office, and an airstrip. The town is packed this night. Friends and family from all over Alaska have come to Tanana to attend Maud's potlatch.

The first part of the potlatch is held at Maud's house the next day. By the time we arrive, over a hundred people are already there, sitting on benches and chairs facing a makeshift stage. As we search for a seat, a slight, middle-aged man is speaking into the microphone. Wearing a navy suit jacket over neatly pressed blue jeans, he is describing some mischief he and Maud got into as children. As he talks, people with pots

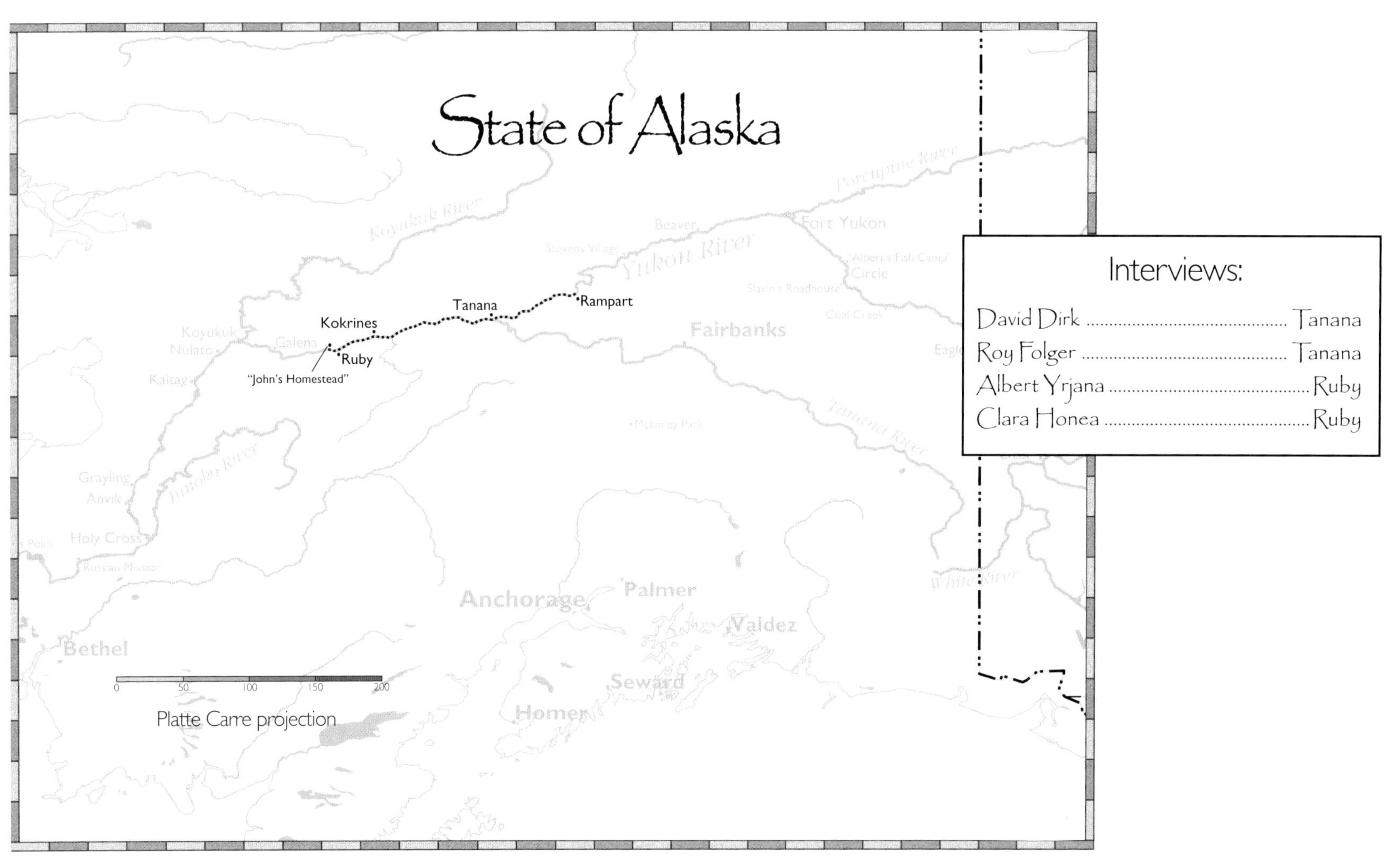
State of Alaska
Rampart
Tanana
Kokrines
Ruby
"John's Homestead"
Fort Yukon
Beaver
Yukon River
Porcupine River
Circle
Fairbanks
Galena
Koyukuk
Nulato
Kaltag
Grayling
Anvik
Holy Cross
Bethel
Anchorage
Palmer
Valdez
Seward
Homer
Tanana River
White River
0 50 100 150 200
Platte Carre projection
Interviews:
David Dirk .... Tanana
Roy Folger .... Tanana
Albert Yrjana .... Ruby
Clara Honea .... Ruby

of food push through the crowd and serve the seated people. Above, the summer sky is a piercing blue with high, puffy clouds drifting lazily towards the north. Roughened by the wind, waves on the river glitter in the sun. When the crowd starts laughing uproariously at the end of the story, I forget for a moment we are at a funeral.

When the service ends a few hours later, people drift toward the community hall. Many have changed into traditional clothes: the women wear jewel-bright dresses and embroidered moccasins, and have tied leather thongs in their tightly braided hair, while the men have donned colorful tunics over their everyday clothes. With his long braid swinging, one man walks to the community hall wearing a fringed, butter-colored skin shirt over a pair of buckskin trousers. A Harley-Davidson kerchief is knotted at his throat.

In the hall, an elder beats a fast rhythm on a circular drum while singing an Indian song in a high, nasal voice. Except for the row of elders sitting at the front of the hall and the few who cling self-consciously to the periphery (me and Kathleen), everyone dances. They dance until, several hours later, people start pushing through the crowd with platters of sandwiches. Once supper is finished, gifts are distributed: everything from shovels and blankets to fabric and coffee pots.

"How can people afford all this?" I ask Martin who has a new red blanket tucked under his arm.

"They can't, really," he answers. "People go in debt over these potlatches. But it's important to the family to throw a really big party when someone dies. They want the person who is gone to be remembered well."

Believing that potlatches encouraged a non-European system of values regarding property—where goods were given away rather than accumulated—they were banned both in Canada and the United States in the late 1800s. Also, it was believed that moving children from village to village to attend potlatches spread sickness and disrupted schooling, and that native women, needing money for potlatch goods, went to the cities and became prostitutes.[1]

The ban was lifted many years later, when the significance of the potlatch in Indian traditional life was finally recognized. Today, many people in northern communities, particularly the young, have begun asking their elders about the "old ways." In Tanana, the elders are kept particularly busy with questions.

Kathleen and I walk back to the tent in the peach-colored twilight, each carrying two bolts of cotton fabric and some colorful hair ribbons, and followed by the twang of an electric guitar and an occasional shout. I can't help comparing this funeral to my grandmother's. In Tanana, Maud was a well loved and respected Athabaskan elder whose presence and voice would long be missed. In Trenton, Ontario, my dear grandmother was one of our society's ignored and forgotten.

The service for my grandmother was held in a funeral home. In the small, airless room, the walls, carpeting, seat covers, and draperies were a uniform beige. Bouquets of stiff, waxy-looking flowers surrounded her casket at the front of the room. Besides our small family, the only others attending were a band of very old people who listened to the minister's perfunctory service with sad, rounded shoulders. At the graveside, standing next to the priest, I saw stuck to the open page from the Bible a cheery, yellow post-it note with my grandmother's name on it.

---

[1] Nancy Baele, "Artifacts of the Once-Banned Potlatch Are at the Hull Museum," *Montreal Gazette*, January 7, 1995.

Dearest Mo + Kath,

You are two of the sweetest gals I've ever had the privilege of knowing. Sorry we had to part so soon but I have a good reason to check out Montreal again. I'm looking forward to it. Thanks for your kindness and God bless you both.

Your Fiddler
on the Yukon,

Marty

P.S. Stay here as long as you like. Lock up when you leave.

Residents along the Yukon graciously opened their doors to us, as attested to by this good-bye note from Martin Bradley.

August 12

David Dirk
Tanana, AK

David was born in Frankfurt, Germany, in 1969. He began the trip down the Yukon River on his raft in 1990. We met him and his girlfriend, Isabel, during his third summer on the river.

A log raft

The best logs you can get are fire killed logs that are still standing. On Lake Bennett there were about 15 of them and they were pretty good size. I cut them with an axe, not a chain saw. We built the raft in the water because you can move the logs around easily. We spent three weeks putting the raft together. If it's windy and the waves are high, it gives me that feeling like the ocean. Sometimes we take watches. Sometimes you have to be very concentrated. The advantage is we have the mast. We can climb up and look ahead. They had log rafts in the Middle Ages in Germany too.

The drifting feeling

In a way local people look down at you. They call you drifter. They're scared about drifting people. Drifting is completely different than being in the canoe. It's that drifting feeling, slowly going along. We can cook on the raft. We can sleep on the raft. It's nice, you know, the life we have out here. Camping and living basic.

Don't have a future

I would say that of the people I met, they don't have a future. Alaska is not a place where you think about the future. You just live every day. It's the wilderness.

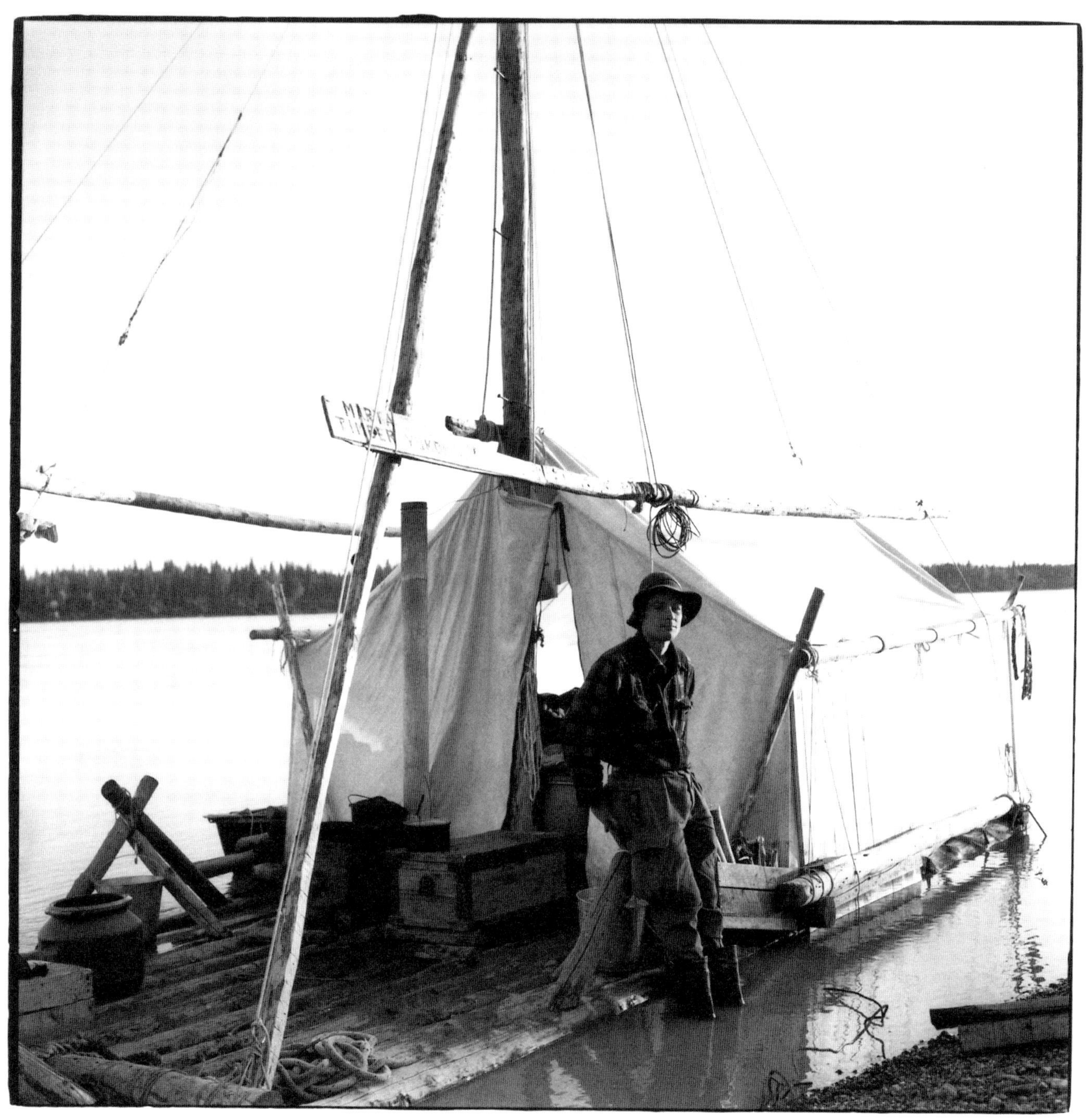

August 14

Roy Folger
Tanana, AK

Roy was born in a fish camp along the Tanana River, and was in the service from 1944 to 1947, then again from 1960 to 1964. In 1956, he and his wife Pinky were married. He was a government laborer from 1965 until he retired in 1986.

The dance

One winter we were cutting wood at our camp. This one wood cutting day, there was a dance the next night in Tanana. I asked the old man if I could take the dog team and go down to Tanana. It was 44 miles by trail. He said they needed the dogs the next day. So, the next morning I got up early and started cutting wood. I cut wood until three o'clock that afternoon, then I put on my running moccasins, had a little snack, and I took off. Pretty good trail. Seven hours I was in Tanana. I ran all the way. I was going to the dance! I was 16 or 17, somewhere in there. I danced all night.

The return

Next morning, I ate breakfast and took off back up to the camp. It took me nine hours to go back up. I run and walk. I mostly walk, but I run to keep awake. Rub snow in my face.

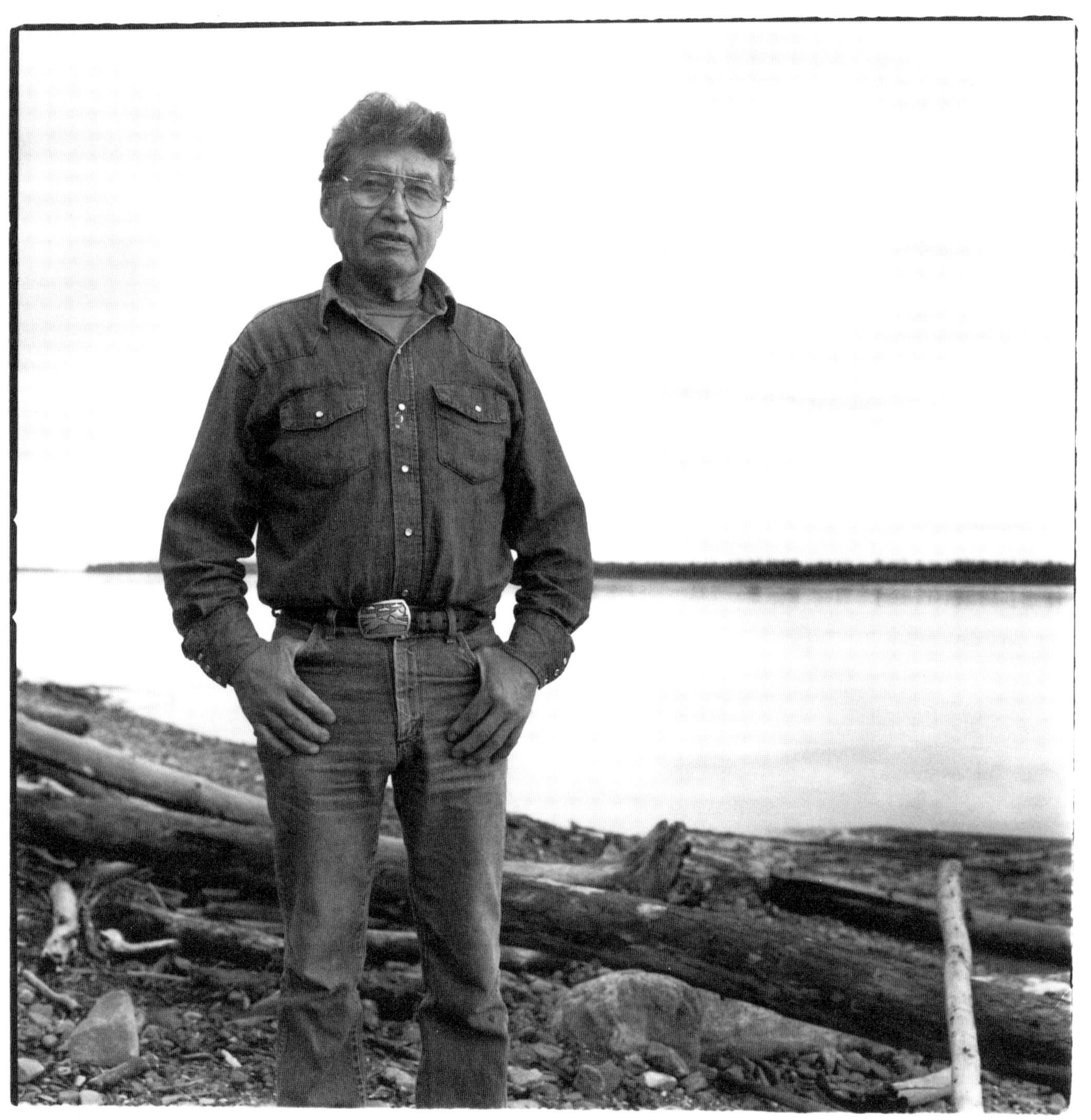

August 17

Albert Yrjana
Ruby, AK

Albert was born in 1910 on a Finnish commune in Michigan. From the time he was a boy, he wanted to go to Alaska. He arrived in 1935. In 1938, Albert moved to Ruby where he still lives today. As well as working for the road commission, he has been a trapper, fisherman, miner, and sawmill owner. Albert is a widower.

His obsession

I couldn't get here in '33. The depression was on. I tried to make it, but I had only two and a half dollars in my pocket. I got as far as Wyoming, then my money was gone, so I had to go back home. Then, in '35, it had let up a little and I got a job in a logging camp driving horses. I worked the winter and I had almost a hundred dollars saved. That's what I came to Alaska with.

When I got here, it was like I was home. That's why I won't leave unless in a box. It was my dream or obsession or whatever you call it. That's what I wanted to do. And I did it. I've been here now for quite awhile.

There's fish in the river and meat in the woods. If you need a few dollars, you set up your traps. I trapped for 40 years. It was a nice life. My wife was used to that life. Frontier life. She even learned trapping. She wouldn't stay in town while I was on the trapline. She wanted to be out doing the cooking, keep the fire going. We had a good working arrangement.

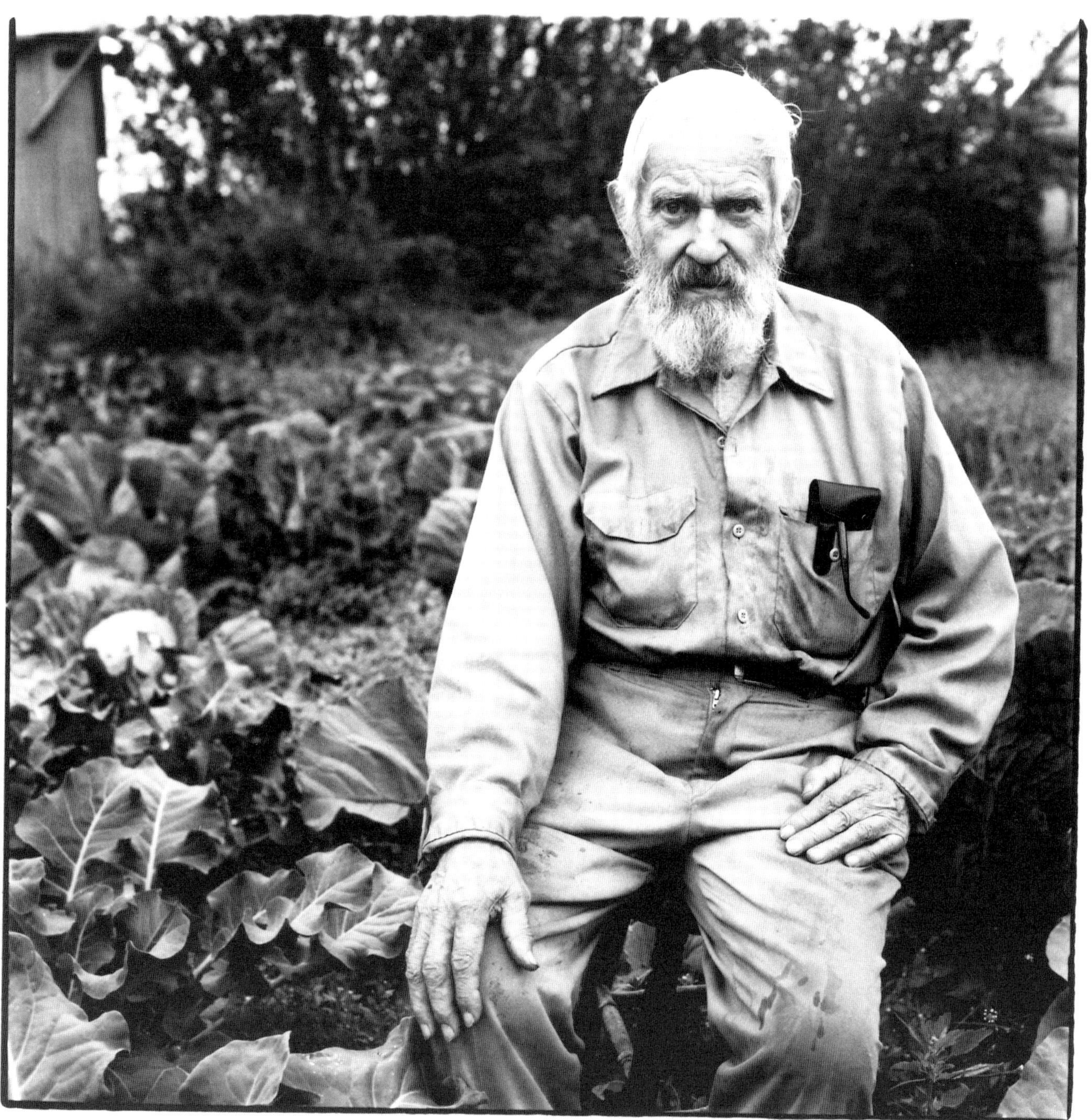

August 18

Clara Honea
Ruby, AK

Clara was born in 1930 in the Ruby area and married in 1947. She and her husband had 14 children. Clara worked as a nurse's aide from 1971 to 1986.

The big open place

I watch break-up every year. To me it's kind of sad because one of my boys, five years ago, he drowned about two miles down the river. Everybody was going to Galena for something, maybe basketball, on snow machines. It was really late and really stormy that night. He took off ahead of everybody else. He went straight down the middle of the Yukon and he forgot about that open place. He drove into that big open place. And so when the ice goes out I feel really sad. I feel sad about it.

Years ago when the river froze, you were never supposed to go across until an elder went across with a long pole and an axe and made this one trail across the river. Now I notice that after the river freezes up, people are out there like pups, just going anywhere. I don't think that they're respecting the river. Even my son wasn't.

The river

I've lived on this river all my life. I just can't imagine living anywhere else. I love to watch it when the ice is moving in the spring time. I like to sit on the bank and just watch the river. It's just something I just wish everybody in the world could see.

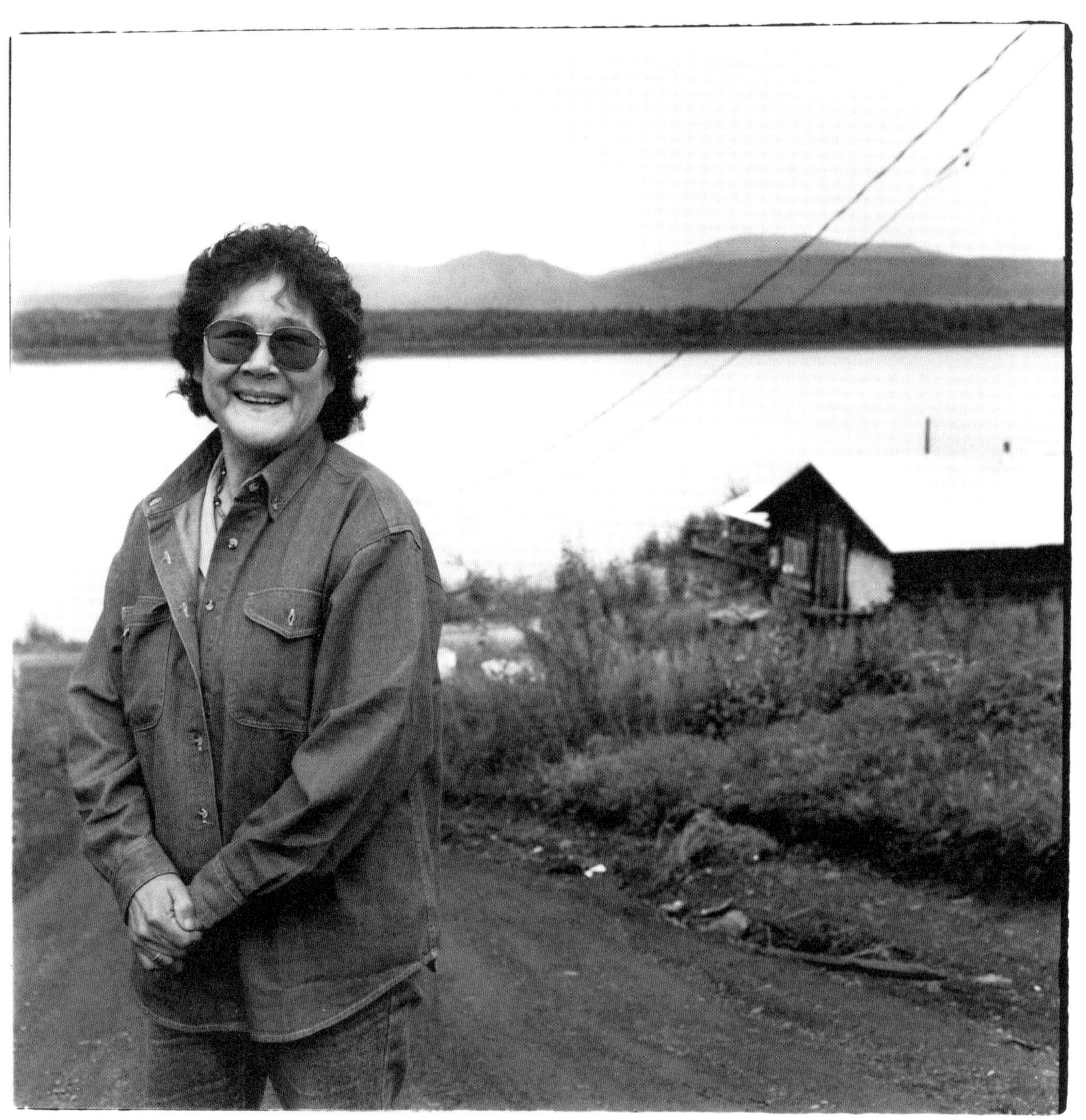

John's Homestead to Grayling, Alaska

"My Heart" Milepost 1,264, John's Homestead • *The Regina Hotel*

The woman is framed by piles of ruby colored salmon as we paddle by the homestead. She is cutting fish into strips at a rough table by the river. In the clearing behind her, a tall windmill spins in the wind, smoke rises in cottony puffs from a large cabin, and beds of bright flowers dot the clearing like scatter rugs.

"Hey, how are you!" the woman calls, waving her filleting knife as we beach the canoe nearby. Finishing a large fish with quick slices, she takes off her gloves and yellow apron, and tosses them on the blood-soaked table. She rubs her heavily pregnant belly as she walks towards us.

"Hi! I'm Linda Nylunsing! Who are you?" A tall, blond woman in her late thirties, her Dutch accent reminds me immediately of my relatives, and, for a moment, I see the smiling, leathery faces of my Tante Sus and my Tante Trinke.

After introducing ourselves, I say, "We met your friend, Len, in Ruby yesterday. He said to say 'Hi' for him if we stopped here."

"Oh, that's nice," Linda says with a wide smile. "Come on up to the cabin. Can you stay for supper tonight?"

"That would be great!" says Kathleen, faking surprise. Len assured us we would be invited for dinner.

Following Linda into the cabin, we walk into a warm yeasty cloud. "Smells like the bread's almost done," she says, peering into the cookstove. "No—not quite." Then she leans out the kitchen window and bellows, "Hey, John! We've got visitors!"

"Oh! Very nice to meet you," John says, towering over us. Thrusting out a bony hand, he says, "Friends of Len's, are you? Canoeing to the sea? Wonderful! I want to hear all about it." Then he looks at his watch and says, "It will have to wait until supper, though. I'm right in the middle of something. Well, nice to met you. See you at supper!" Then the screen door slams behind him and he is gone.

"That's John for you—always in a hurry," Linda explains, pouring boiling water into a teapot. "In the summer, he has so many projects on the go—sometimes I hardly see him for days."

Holding a steaming mug of tea between her work-worn hands, she tells us she has been living with John for two years. She likes homesteading, but she misses many things too. The company of women, for example, especially now with the baby coming—there are so many things she doesn't know.

John, she says, came from the "lower 48," and has been homesteading on the Yukon for nearly 20 years. A hunter, trapper, and fisherman, John lives almost completely off the land. He has no desire to leave the bush.

"You should have seen him in Holland—he talked about Alaska the whole time!" Linda says, rolling her eyes.

As the sun drops behind the trees across the river, Linda says, "I can't believe I've been here all afternoon—I must have needed to talk. I really do miss female companionship."

As we follow Linda out to the garden to pick vegetables for a salad, I think how easily this life could have been mine.

"I want to go to photography school in Montreal. Do you want to come with me?" I ask David. It is September 4, 1989, at 11:50 am. We are sitting on the grass in front of Gold City Tours, Dawson's travel agency.

"I don't want to live in the city—I want to be out on the trapline. If you want to be with me, that's where I'll be," he answers stubbornly.

To make late registration for the photography program at Montreal's Concordia University, I have to leave Dawson by 12:00. At 11:55, I am still undecided. At 11:57, I hand $900 to

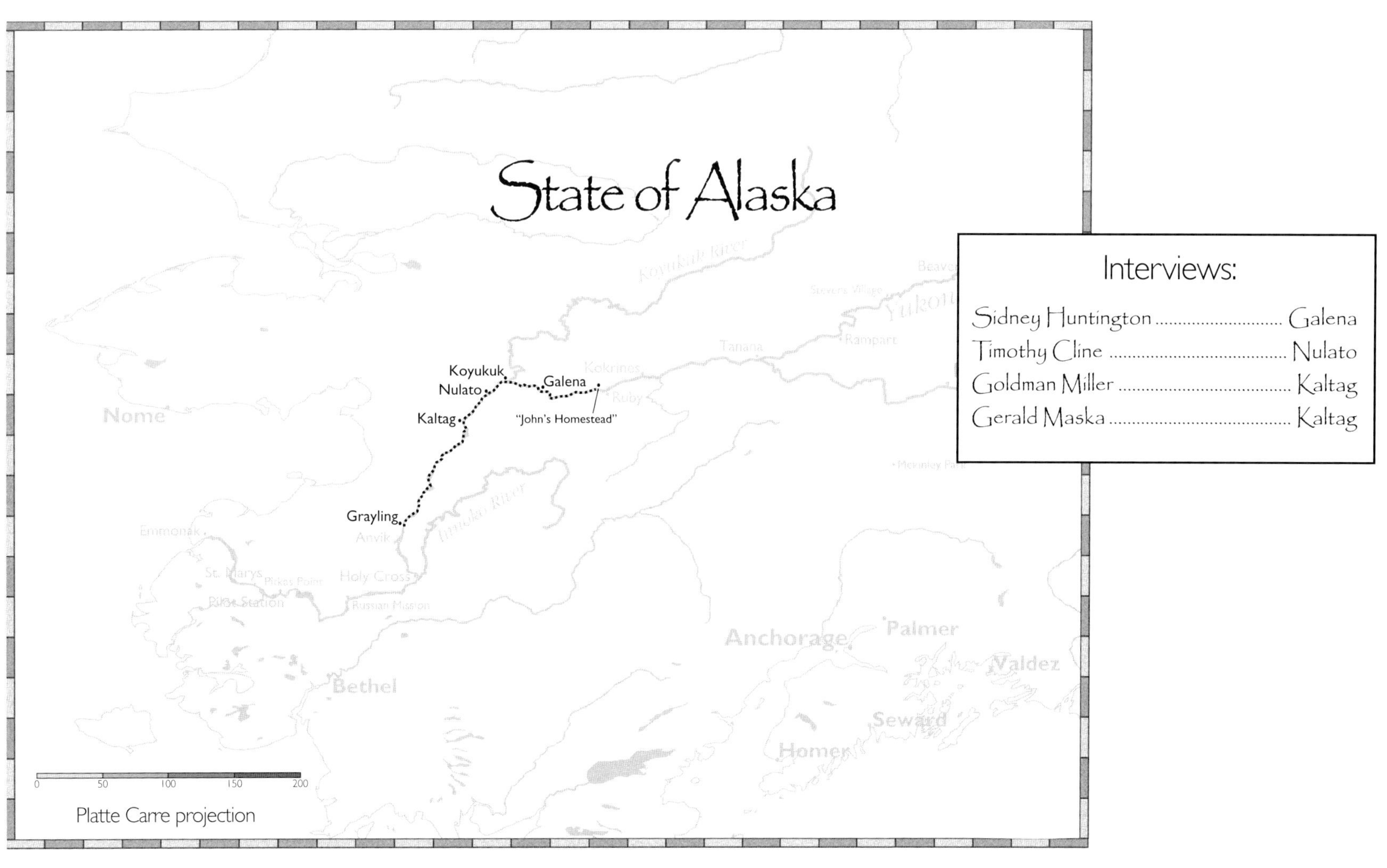

State of Alaska
Koyukuk
Nulato
Galena
Kaltag
"John's Homestead"
Grayling
Nome
Bethel
Anchorage
Palmer
Valdez
Seward
Homer
0 50 100 150 200
Platte Carre projection
Interviews:
Sidney Huntington .... Galena
Timothy Cline .... Nulato
Goldman Miller .... Kaltag
Gerald Maska .... Kaltag

the travel agent at Gold City Tours. Dawson is a colorful speck beneath my plane a half hour later.

I will change planes three times before reaching Montreal. On the Dawson-Whitehorse leg of my journey, I am euphoric: I have made the right decision. I am going to school! At the beginning of my Whitehorse-Vancouver leg, I am not so sure. Did I make the right decision? Is school really that important? What about David? When the plane's wheels hit Vancouver airport's tarmac, my certainty has crumbled completely. I find the Canadian Airlines ticket counter in the Vancouver terminal. Feigning nonchalance, I hand my ticket to an agent, and ask her to change my destination from Montreal back to Dawson.

"It'll cost you," the woman says, her bored, tanned face registering no interest or surprise. I wonder how often she has done this.

Back in Dawson, I waitress for a month in the Midnight Sun Tavern to recoup the money I spent on my round trip to the Vancouver airport, but it is worth it. I am at peace. School can wait for another year. I am going into the bush with the man I love.

On the trapline, the battle soon begins. Half of me is deeply in love while the other half mourns the death of my future. Life in the bush is rugged and hard, but is also beautifully simple. I want to be with David, but I also want to go to photography school. David begins to watch me with troubled eyes.

"Just try to be happy about being here," he says. "If you don't, you'll look back on this period of your life and regret it."

In early January, I realize I am pregnant. A few weeks later, I arrive in Dawson with 13 marten pelts in my suitcase. Fred, the wide-girthed owner of Arctic Drugs, gives me $800 for them—enough money to go see the doctor in Whitehorse. I get a ride to Whitehorse with Betty and her seven children. Betty drops me off at the Regina Hotel and says she'll be back in a few days to pick me up.

Lying on the lumpy bed, I scan the hotel room's cracked green walls and pretend I am considering keeping the baby. Tears slide onto the pink and orange petals of the garishly flowered bedspread as I dream about our new life. We'll have a nice little family in the bush—we'll trap and fish! I'll have a garden and I'll even learn to cook better—I owe David that anyway—and I'll put off photography school for a little while longer—Yeah! Everything is going to be just fine. When I picture washday, the dream fades at the edges like an old photograph—a sodden, steaming row of diapers hangs on a clothesline that stretches across the cabin. The baby, covered in sawdust from playing in the wood box, is trying to drink the gray water that pools on the rough, wood floor beneath the diapers.

There are complimentary Gideon Bibles in every room of the Regina Hotel. The book smells of fall leaves as I flip through the pages. When the book doesn't explain why wilderness life often brings out the best in men while it can dwarf and enslave women, I return it to the drawer of the fake wood desk. I need to go to bed. Tomorrow is going to be a long day.

A year after our canoe trip, a friend wrote to say that John and Linda had broken up and that she had gone back to Holland with the baby.

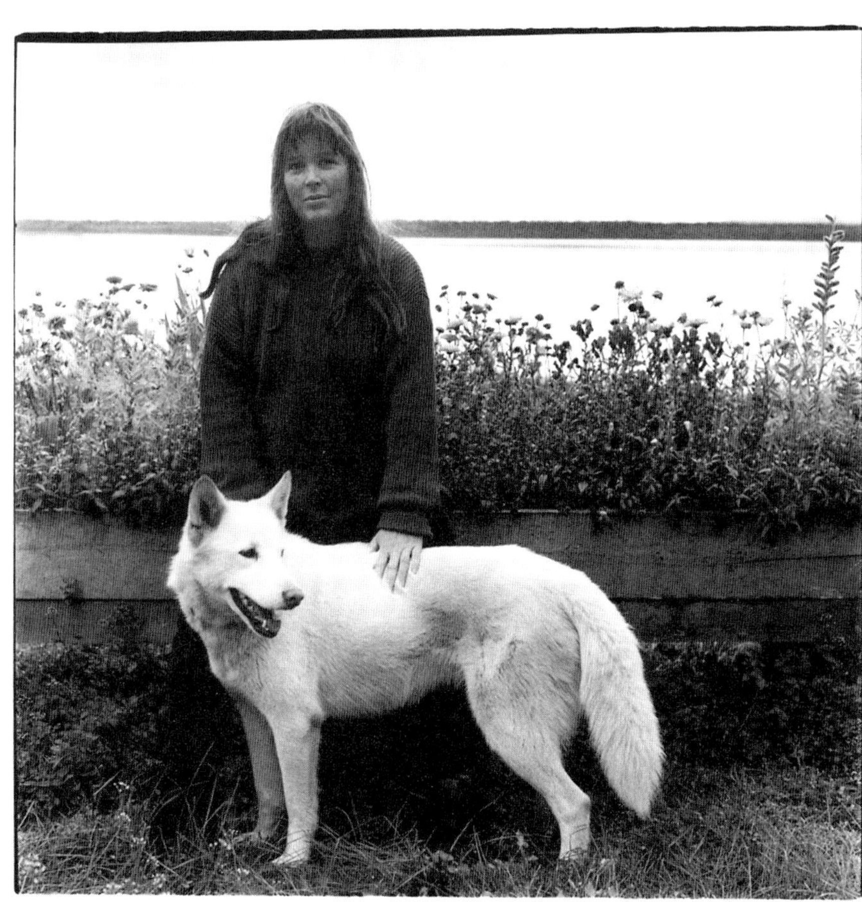

Linda Nylunsing

August 21

Sidney Huntington
Galena, AK

See Sidney Huntington biography, page 103.

The old days

If I could tell my great grandfather that I was going to have a TV and all that crap, he'd say "You're crazy." What did they have? A little mud igloo, no floor in it, no stove—just a little fire in the middle of the place—and they were living on the side where there was no smoke. They had to go outdoors to enjoy life. Back then we weren't living too long.

First moose

When there were no white people here, and nobody managing the resources, there was very little other than just fish. The Indians ate themselves out of house and home. First moose they see on the Koyukuk River was taken by Chief John. They killed it. They needed that pregnant cow moose. Not so much for the meat, but the hide for clothes and what not. That's how they lived—from hand to mouth. We don't have to do that anymore.

Beaver hunting

I saw my aunt taking live beavers out of their house. You wouldn't believe it. She'd chop a hole in the house and go in there and take a live beaver out. She got a hold of that beaver by the front teeth and she passed him right up by her face, over and backwards, then hit him with the flat of the axe. Kill him. Beaver weighs over ninety pounds. Sixty pounds anyway. She took all six of them out of there.

She says, "You want to try it?"

I reluctantly say, "Yes."

She says, "You want to try it? You scared?"

I say, "Yeah, I am."

She says, "If you're a little bit scared, you'll get hurt."

"You take the old ones out first. They behave themselves. The old ones go through, the little ones figure it's O.K. You touch the little ones first they'll nail you."

How many thousands of years did it take them to learn that? Me, I want to be 500 yards away with a big gun.

Spring cleaning

I like to go out and watch break-up. People say "You gotta get away from that ice and high water!" I say that's part of life. It isn't all a bed of roses. Nobody's life is. If there aren't a few hardships along the road—a few bumps—you don't enjoy the damn thing. What the hell better excuse is there for a cleanup in the springtime? Me, I go out there and put everything up on the roof and throw away all my scraps and everything—clean everything up—I'm all ready before the flood comes in. It never materializes, but I'm all cleaned up. It's just a way of life. You've gotta prepare for that sucker.

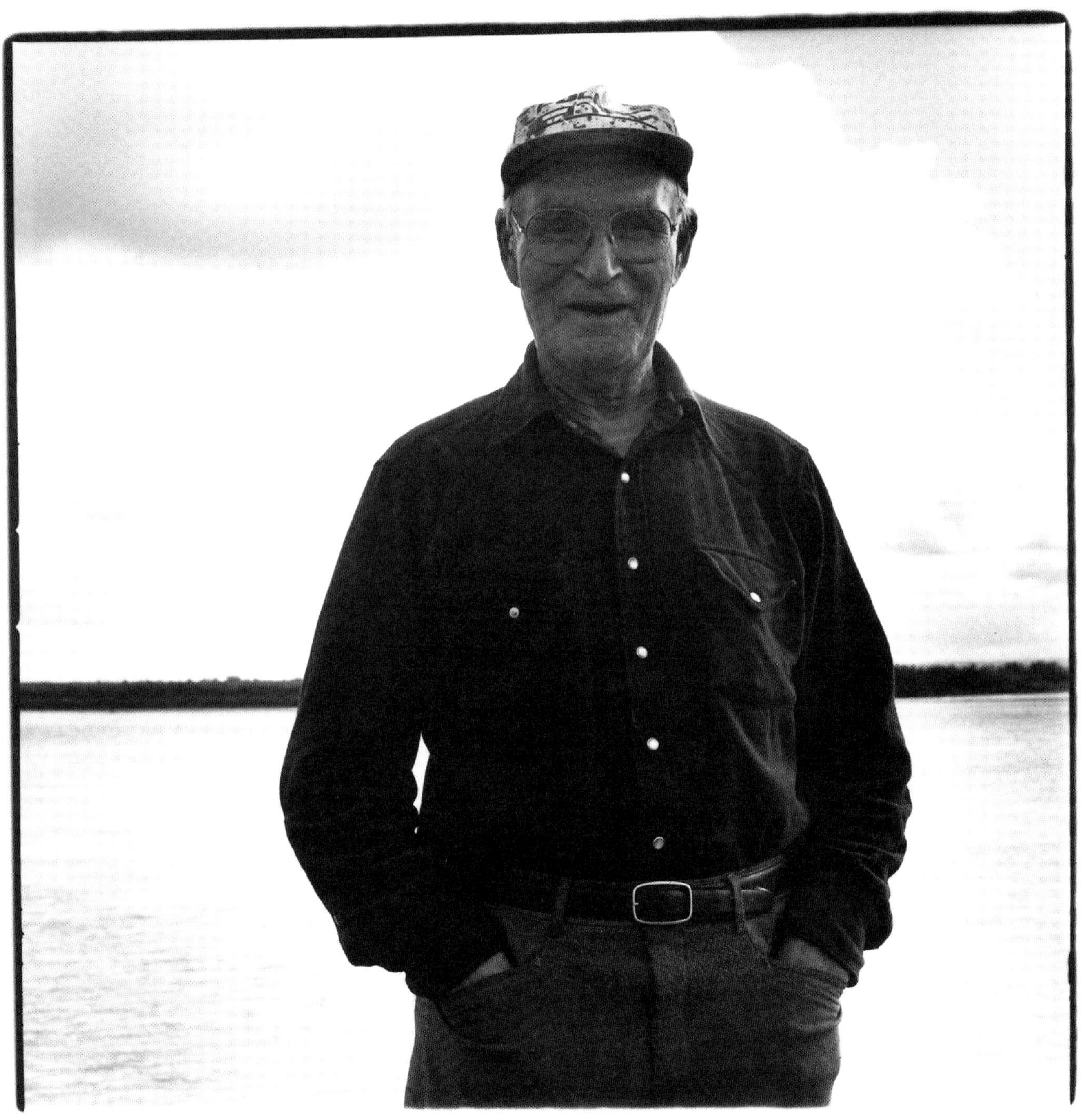

August 26

Timothy Cline
Nulato, AK

Tim was born in 1957 in Santa Rosa, California. He attended college in Tacoma, Washington, receiving a degree in Choral Music Education. In January 1980, he was hired to teach music in Nulato. In 1982, Tim married a local girl, Thelma. They have four children. Tim is now the principal of the Nulato school.

Two worlds

When we open the front doors of our school, the children step from one world into the next. While the students are in the school, they're in a modern educational setting. And they step out of that when they go home. They may have to cut wood and bring water home and clean fish. They live very much in two different worlds. We had to close that gap a little bit. We need to do more schooling in the community. The kids are at fish camp at Bishop Mountain as we speak. Next week, the kids are going 22 miles up the river behind Ruby to camp and to be out in the outdoors. In two weeks, we're sending a group of kids out into the Flats to hunt for moose. While they're doing those things, they'll have a journal and they'll write their experiences. It's just a wonderful tool. It has the potential to be successful if we continue. If we don't, we tear away at their identity.

The future

My sense is that the future is well in hand with these children. No one is going to pull the wool over their eyes. And that's not just the school's doing. That's also the adults and the elders in the community.

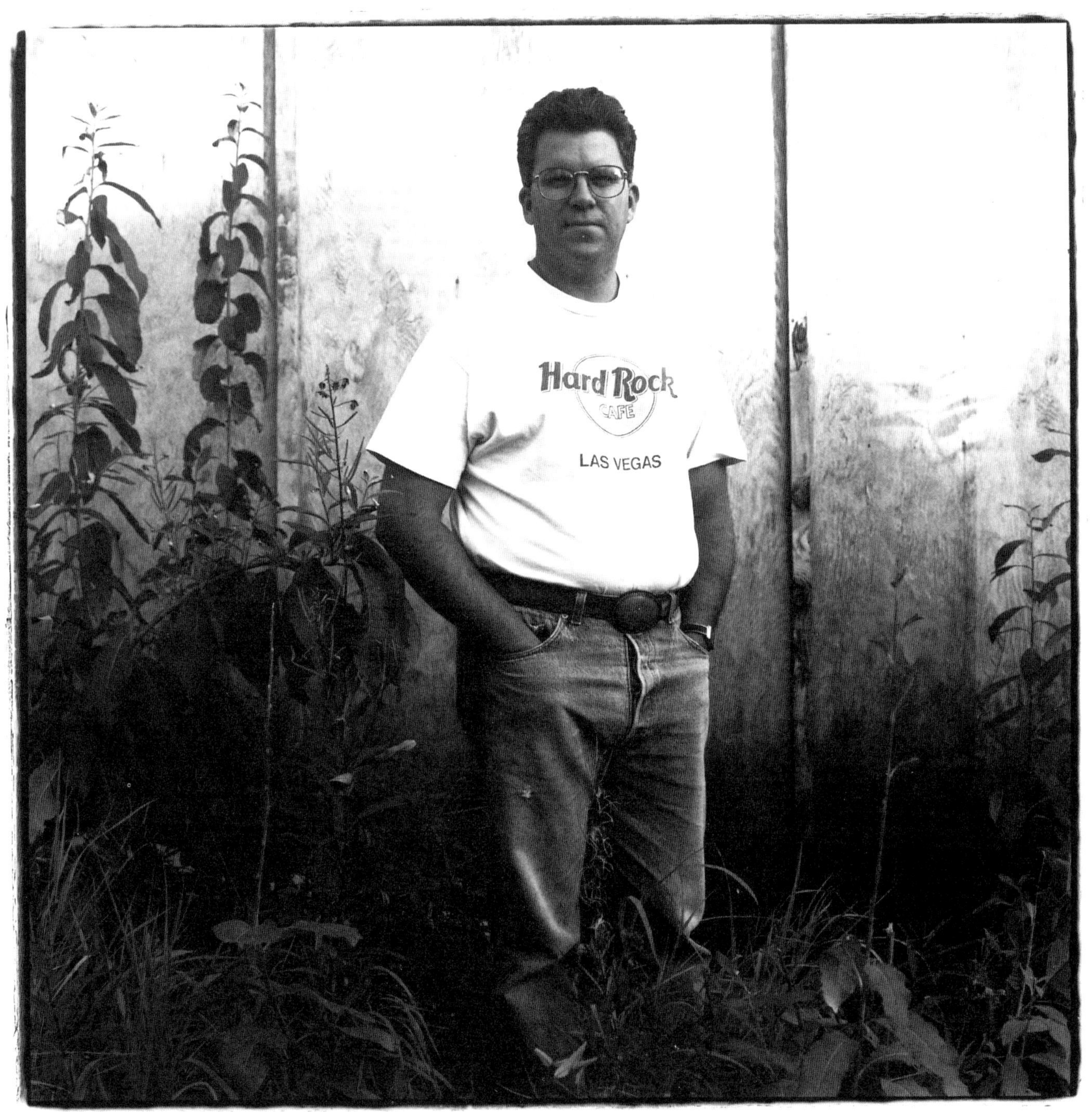
Hard Rock
CAFE
LAS VEGAS

August 28

Goldman Miller
Kaltag, AK

Goldman was born in California in 1962. When she was six, her family moved to Anchorage. They stayed only a short time before returning to the "lower 48." In 1982, Goldman came back to Alaska on her own and spent a few years working on fishing boats. On one of these boats she met a New Zealander, Josh Miller, whom she married in 1984. In 1989, the year Goldman became pregnant with their first child, her husband secured a teaching position in Kaltag, Alaska. The family, with the addition of their second child, has lived in Kaltag ever since.

Questions

If you're new in town—and it doesn't matter if you're white or native—the kids want to know everything about you. I was as big as a house—I was seven months pregnant. The kids—Oh my goodness. We'd come home and there were 15 or 20 kids in the house, running all over the place. Just so excited, asking every possible question. Where do you sleep? Who do you sleep with? How did you meet Josh? How did you get the name Goldman? What are you going to name the baby? Everything. So curious.

Taking care

The thing I love most about living in Kaltag are the people. So generous, they share everything. They share everything they have. I don't think they save money here. The whole reason they save money is just so they can give it away again. It's true of food. No one is allowed to go hungry. If a family is in need, someone will drop off a hind-quarter of meat and not ask for anything in return. You're taken care of. That's the way it is here. People take care. The thing we can learn about their culture is how to share. It's so unquestioned.

Eighty below zero

I've been here when it was 80 below zero, and, on days like that, the smoke from your wood stove and all the smoke from the village just cascades down the riverbank and down on the river. It's like a living thing. When you walk outside, the sound of the snow under your feet is like Styrofoam and the sun is an apricot-colored ball. There's no warmth in it at all. You can't feel it on your face, even a little bit. It's a dim ball in the sky.

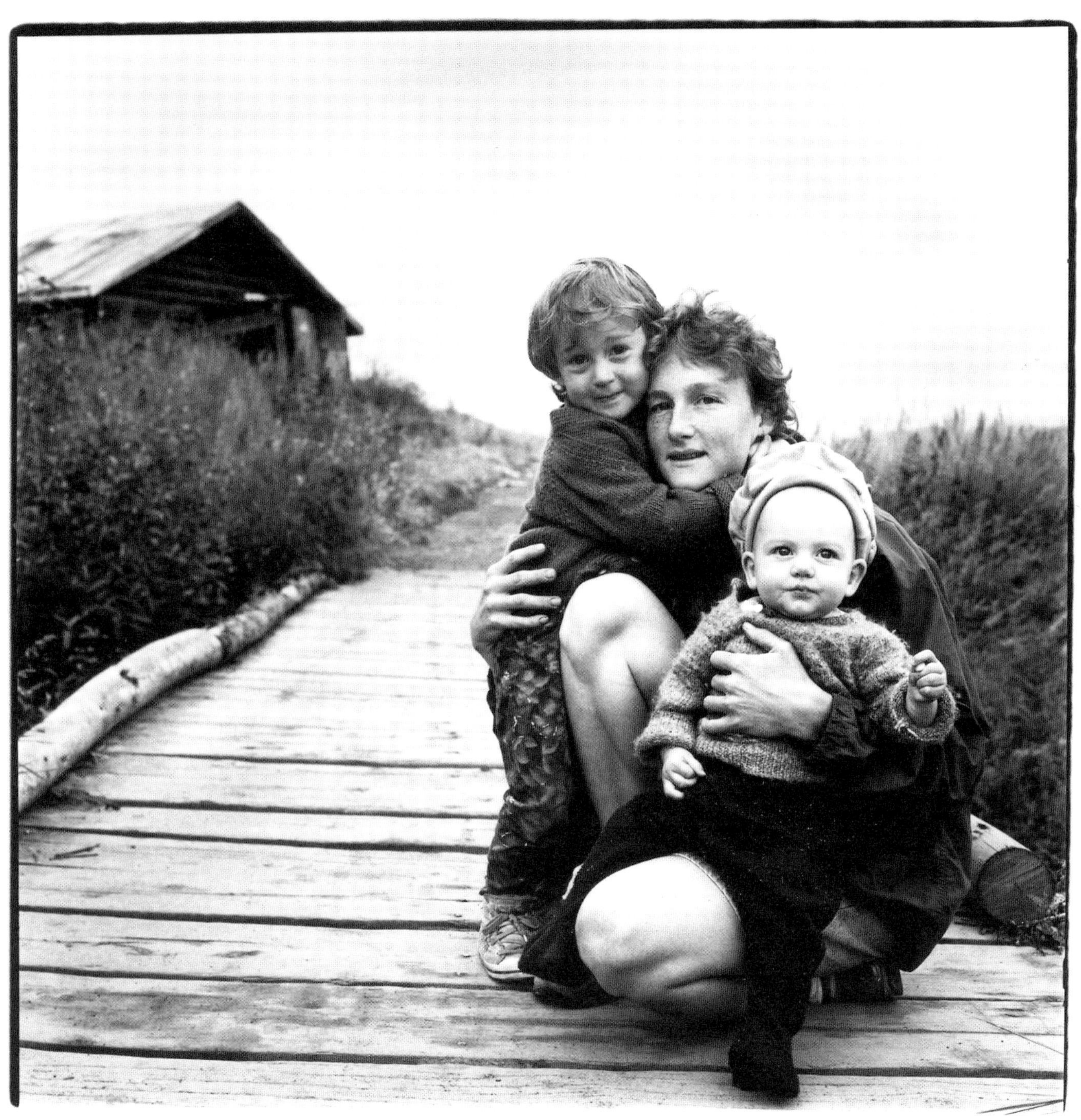

August 28

Gerald Maska
Kaltag, AK

Gerald was born June 30, 1975, and raised in Kaltag, Alaska. He has joined the U.S. Marine Corps and will leave in January for boot camp in California.

Why his gramma took him

Up until I was five, I was living with my parents, but my gramma took me because she didn't want me to stay with them. My mum was an alcoholic and my dad is an alcoholic. He gets kind of pretty much violent when he drinks. Now he's in jail. So she took me. If I hadn't come along, then she probably would have died a long time ago 'cause she wouldn't have had nobody to take care of. And if she hadn't come along, I would have died a long time ago 'cause my parents would have let me die.

When my gramma was young, you kept a kid because that kid would work for you. And she expects me to work, work, work. Chop wood, cut wood, shovel snow, wash dishes, sweep the floor, clean the house. That's the way it was in the olden days. In order to survive, you had to bust your ass. That's not true today, but I know she's trying to teach me—I mean, old people, they didn't get old by being lucky. They get old by knowing what they're doing. And so, you got to listen to them. That's one thing you got to do is to listen to old people.

Valhalla

My life is so fucked up right now. The only thing I got going for me is the Marine Corps. I didn't graduate from high school. I'm not in very good shape. My hair is all fucked up. And so I don't have really much to live for. Except for the Marine Corps. I'm hoping they'll send me overseas to Somalia or the Persian Gulf or Bosnia. Some place where I can get some fighting in.

When I die, I want to go to Valhalla. Where you eat all day, feast all night, get laid and party. Where you fight all day, forever.

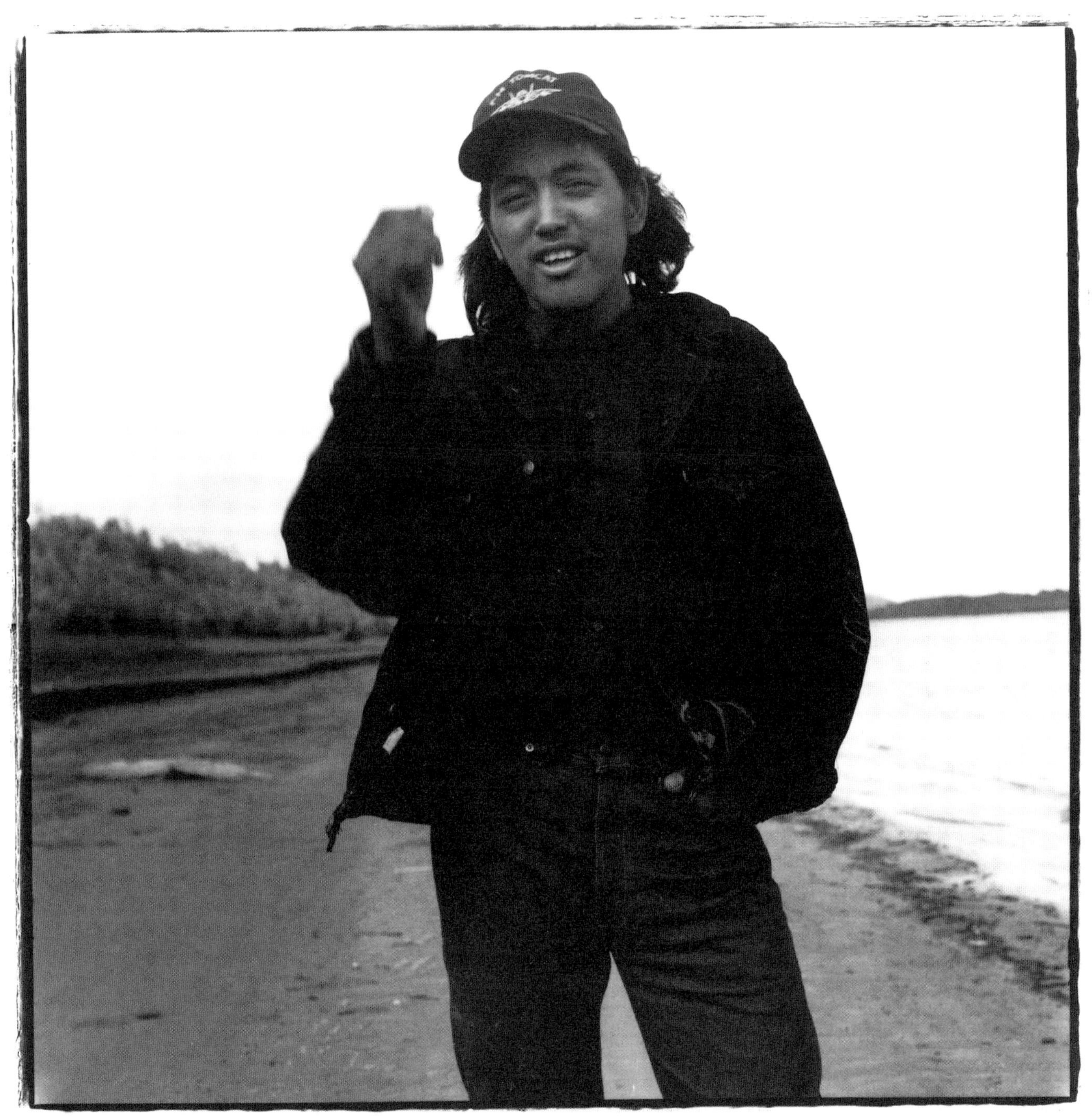

Grayling to Pilot Station, Alaska

"My Heart" Milepost 1,530, Grizzly Bear Campsite • *Faye's Bear Attack*

"They say Faye was sleeping like a baby when the bear ripped through the side of her tent," I tell Kathleen at breakfast in a cafe in Circle. Pausing to carpet a slice of toast with scrambled eggs, I continue: "I heard the story when I was living in Dawson. Faye and her husband were in town for the music festival when they ran into Billy Borishenko. Billy invited them to his fish camp after the festival. That night, the bear ripped through the side of Faye's tent, grabbed her by the head, and dragged her over to a big patch of roses. It rolled her around in the prickles for awhile—wanted to tenderize her a little, they say—then it went back for her husband." Stopping for a moment to wipe my plate with my last piece of toast, I finish, "and that's when Billy blasted that bear with a shotgun."

When we interview her later that day, Faye traces the deep groove in her cheek with her fingertips and says, "This is the best the plastic surgeons could do." Then she changes the subject. "It was hard adjusting to life in town," she says. "I still really miss being out there." We try to learn more about the mauling, but with no success. The bear attack was only one of her many adventures in the bush.

Faye describes the challenge of running a trapline, and never knowing what kind of year it will be. In the north, she explains, most animals are on a five to ten year population cycle. As well, animal populations are often localized. One valley might be full of beaver, for example, while a valley 50 kilometers away is barren. Cycles of different species may overlap, but these cycles are rarely the same length, making hunting and trapping excellent in some years and scarce in others. Some common northern animals, Faye tells us, are mountain goat and sheep, lynx, wolf, moose, caribou, otter, ermine, weasel, mink, coyote, porcupine, muskrat, rabbit, squirrel, and, of course, black and grizzly bear.

Most animals were hunted by the early Indians and provided clothing, bedding, tents, rope, sinew, needles, and tools. Because the early Indians relied so heavily on animals for their survival, many customs, myths, and rituals developed around them. Success in hunting, the natives believed, depended less on the hunter's skill and more on the animal's willingness to offer itself. For this reason, hunters were extremely modest—being too confident about shooting and trapping abilities didn't show the animals proper respect.

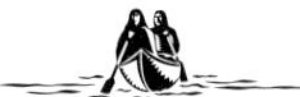

Sidney Huntington talks about some of the old ways of the Koyukon people when we interview him in Galena. When he finishes his beaver hunting story, I ask him to verify an intriguing Koyukon legend.

"If a bear is charging a woman—me for example—is it really true that I'm supposed to pull my pants down, tuck my head between my knees, and point my bum towards the bear?" I ask, feeling utterly ridiculous.

The first time we had heard this was in Stevens Village. "The bear will get embarrassed if you do that," an old native guy had said.

"Yeah, RIGHT!" I had thought to myself.

Then, a few weeks and a couple of hundred miles downriver, another person told us exactly the same thing. "Oh yes," the man said earnestly. "If you do that, the bear will feel ashamed for wanting to attack a woman and he will go away."

"Yup, that's what we believe," says Sidney with a smile, smoothing the lace doily on his armchair with restless fingers. A trim, energetic 78-year-old man with piercing eyes, Sidney sits perfectly erect, leaving a wide gap between his back and the soft, yellow seat cushions. "Women weren't even supposed to talk about the 'big animal,' you know—bad luck," he says. "I write about that in my book."

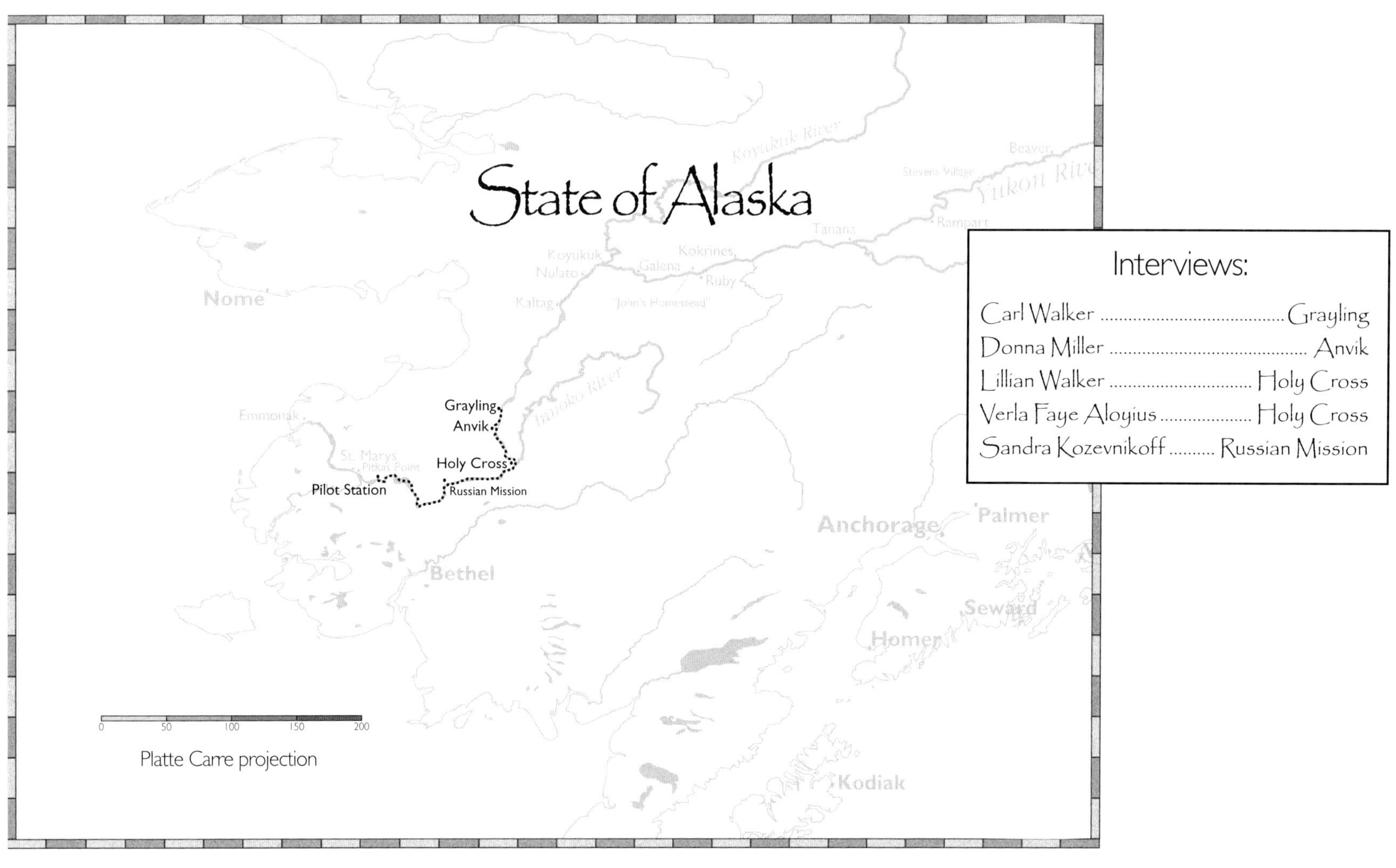
State of Alaska
Interviews:
Carl Walker .... Grayling
Donna Miller .... Anvik
Lillian Walker .... Holy Cross
Verla Faye Aloyius .... Holy Cross
Sandra Kozevnikoff .... Russian Mission
Grayling
Anvik
Holy Cross
Pilot Station
Russian Mission
Nome
Bethel
Anchorage
Palmer
Seward
Homer
Kodiak
Koyukuk
Nulato
Kaltag
Galena
Kokrines
Ruby
Tanana
Rampart
Beaver
Stevens Village
Koyukuk River
Innoko River
Emmonak
St. Marys
Pitkas Point
"John's Homestead"
0 50 100 150 200
Platte Carre projection

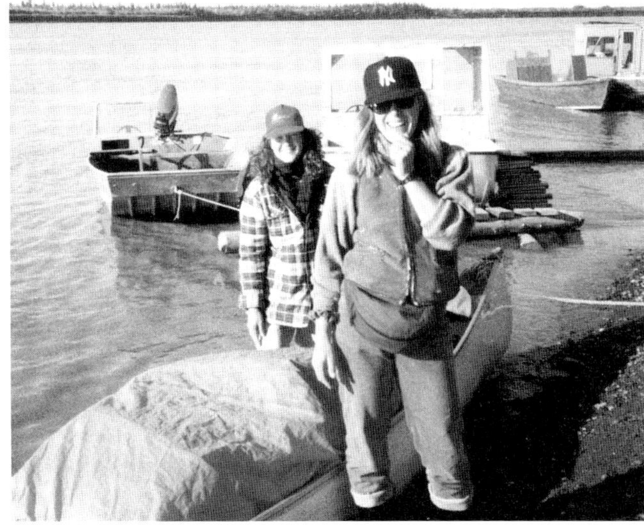

Kathleen and I on the lower Yukon. This photo was snapped by our special friend and benefactor, Trooper Tom, of Galena.

I feel great affection and admiration for Sidney when we leave this remarkable man's house several hours later with signed copies of *Shadows on the Koyukuk.* Half Athabaskan, Sidney Huntington was born and grew up in the Koyukuk River region of northern Alaska. Athabaskan stories, customs, and legends weave seamlessly through his wilderness experiences, creating a broad, rich tapestry of a man completely at home in his environment.

A few days later, the choppy waves are harsh and orange in the low sun when we begin looking for an island to camp on for the night. We prefer camping on small islands rather than the riverbanks, figuring if an island is bear-free when we arrive, chances are good it will stay that way until we leave.

There is no place to stop for the next two hours, then finally, the river splits around a large island. I steer the boat into the protected sloughs hoping to find a sheltered camp spot on the lee side. We scan the impenetrable wall of spruce trees topping the island's impossibly high bank. There is nowhere to stop. Twenty minutes later, the island is a small speck behind us. There are no islands ahead. Then I see an open area on the riverbank beside a swift running stream.

"Hey, Kathleen!" I say. "What do you think about breaking with tradition and camping over there on the riverbank?"

"Why not?" she answers tiredly.

The boat lands with a gentle hiss on the soft, muddy riverbank. I start unloading the boat while Kathleen heads into the bushes for a pee.

"Monique!" Kathleen suddenly yells. "You gotta check this out!"

Kathleen is standing by the creek, looking down at two pairs of fresh grizzly tracks, one large, one small.

Fighting an instinctive urge to run, I bend to get a closer look. Before this, the only grizzly tracks I'd ever seen were homemade—for the fleshy pads on the bear's foot, the side of a clenched fist is pressed into the earth, and five thumbnail impressions were made radiating from the top of the "pad" to suggest a grizzly's lethal claws.

"They look exactly like the fake ones!" I exclaim excitedly.

"That's great, Monique," Kathleen answers shortly, "but these are real—and really fresh too! And it's probably a mother and cub!"

As I decide whether we should stay or paddle on, images of the traditional feminine defense against bear attacks battle with the memory of Faye's bear story.

"Let's get out of here !" I yell, running for the boat.

***Sidney Huntington,** the son of a Klondike gold miner and a Koyukuk Indian, was born in 1915 in Hughes, Alaska. In 1920, after inadvertently eating the liver of a toxic Whitefish, his mother suddenly died at the family's remote home on the Hog River. Because his father was away, five-year-old Sidney had to take care of his three-year-old brother and nine-month-old sister until help arrived two weeks later. This experience left a deep impression on Sidney.*

When not at school at the Holy Cross Mission or the Eklutna Vocational School, Sidney helped his father on the Hog River trapline. After enlisting for World War II, Sidney and his new wife returned to the trapline where they spent the next 15 years.

The Huntington family moved to Galena in 1963. Teaching himself the trade from books, Sidney became a carpenter and worked at the Galena Air Force Base until 1971, when he quit to build a fish processing plant. In its heyday, seven 737 air transports full of Sidney's Yukon River salmon flew out of Galena daily. The plant employed many people from the community until it was closed in 1975 due to prohibitively high shipping costs. A smaller plant was opened in 1988 which is still operational today.

From 1972 to 1987, Sidney was appointed to the Alaska Board of Fish and Game. A strong advocate of local education, Sidney was a member of the Galena School Board for 25 years. Named Conservationist of the Year in 1986 by the Alaska Outdoor Council, Sidney also was named Trapper of the Year by the Fairbanks Trappers Association in the following year. Not to be outdone, the Alaska State Legislature named him Trapper and Conservationist of the Year in 1988.

In recognition of his dedication to his family, community, region, and state, Sidney was awarded the honorary degree of Doctor of Public Service by the University of Alaska in 1989. Sidney's fascinating autobiography, Shadows on the Koyukuk, *was published in 1993.*

September 2

Carl Walker
Grayling, AK

Carl was born in a small community on the Innoko River. After marrying in 1970, he and his wife moved to Grayling. The father of three children, Carl is a trapper, fisherman, and Grayling's mayor.

Their oldest boy

We lost our oldest son to the river. The heck of it was we never thought it would happen to us. Boating accident. Drinking too. That's why we quit drinking. We lost our oldest boy. Eighteen years old. That's something you can't change, you know. Terrible. It seemed like the world just stopped. People talking to you and you don't care who they are. It's there in your head that he's gone.

Peace

They're taking two bodies from the Smithsonian Institution and bringing them back. They were stolen a long time ago by archaeologists. When they do bring the bodies back, we'll put them up there in the graveyard with the other people. There's some more that are still out there. We got to fight for those heads to come back. Thirty or forty of them. Heads. Bones. We want them back so we can bury them in peace. Then, maybe things will be all right again.

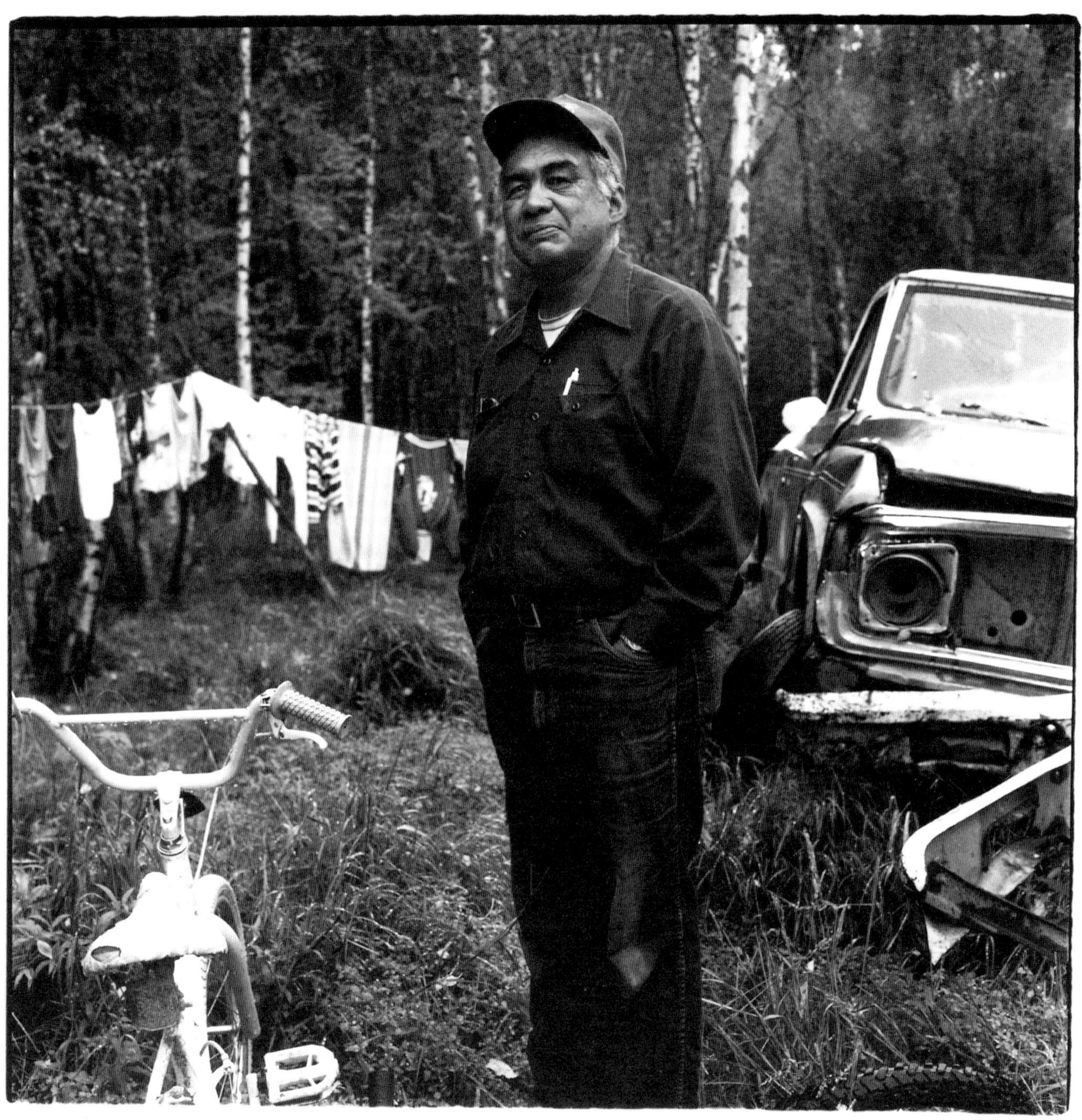

September 3

Donna Miller
Anvik, AK

Donna was born in 1934 and grew up in Simcoe, Ontario. She went to college in Toronto, and in 1953 she and her family moved to Alaska. Donna married a jazz musician in Anchorage and the couple had four children. When the marriage dissolved several years later, Donna moved to Anvik with the children to teach high school. She retired in 1987. Donna now divides her time between the Anvik Historical Society and helping a friend on his trapline.

The wood

My friend, an older native lady, told me I don't know how to split wood.

I said, "I know I don't know how. I always have trouble."

She picked up this log I'd been whacking away on. She turned it over—I mean I'd hit it about 10 times and it wouldn't split—and she said "Hit it there."

I hit it and it split in half. I said, "You must be a medicine woman."

She just chuckled. She said, "I've been splitting wood all my life. I know how to do it."

There's so much you can learn. I'm learning so many things from the elders that the kids are not learning. And that's one of the things that worries me and worries them. Some things are traditional knowledge and some are just basic skills. Like the wood.

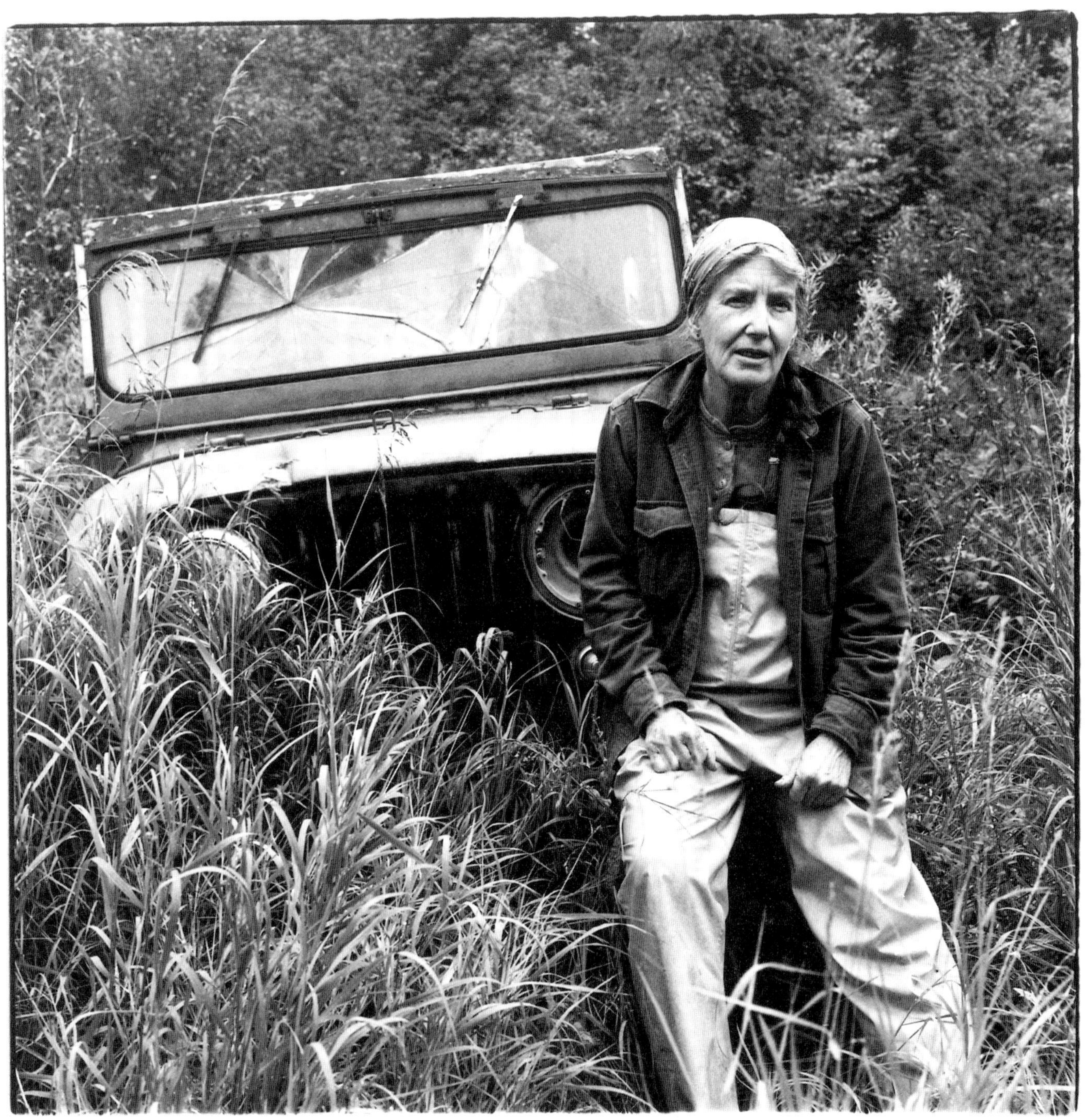

September 6

Lillian Walker
Holy Cross, AK

Lillian Walker was born in Unalakleet, Alaska, in 1924. At the age of 13, she was sent to the mission in Holy Cross for an education. In 1942, she married a local boy, David Walker. They had four children. Lillian is an accomplished midwife and was the health aide in Holy Cross for many years.

The Holy Cross mission

I had just turned 13 when I came to the Holy Cross mission. I was there for five years. It was strict. I guess they had to be to keep everyone in line. I liked it. I learned beadwork and how to sew. I learned to patch clothes very well. I learned how to knit and how to crochet. I hated making socks. They taught us how to cook and they taught us how to sew and how to be clean. If it wasn't for their teaching, we probably wouldn't be what we are today.

What I didn't like about some of the nuns was how they treated the little ones. If they wanted to go to the bathroom at night, they weren't allowed to. So they'd wet their beds. And they'd get a whipping for it. This one boy, every morning he had that wet sheet hung over his head and he had to stand in the corner. The sister that was in charge of those kids, she shouldn't have been. She was a mean one. Really mean. He was just a little one. Six years old.

We could not, no way, speak anything but English. There'd be some kids, they would come in from the villages and they couldn't speak English. They'd punish them. The kids were punished if they spoke their language. Then all of a sudden they want us to get our language back. Strange. Yeah, anyhow, now Holy Cross is practically all English speaking people.

Working for God

A lot of people that were here in the mission didn't want anything to do with the Catholic church because of the way they were treated. I go to church. God didn't do that, they did. Even though they're working for God, or they're suppose to be, they're humans too. And human beings can be cruel.

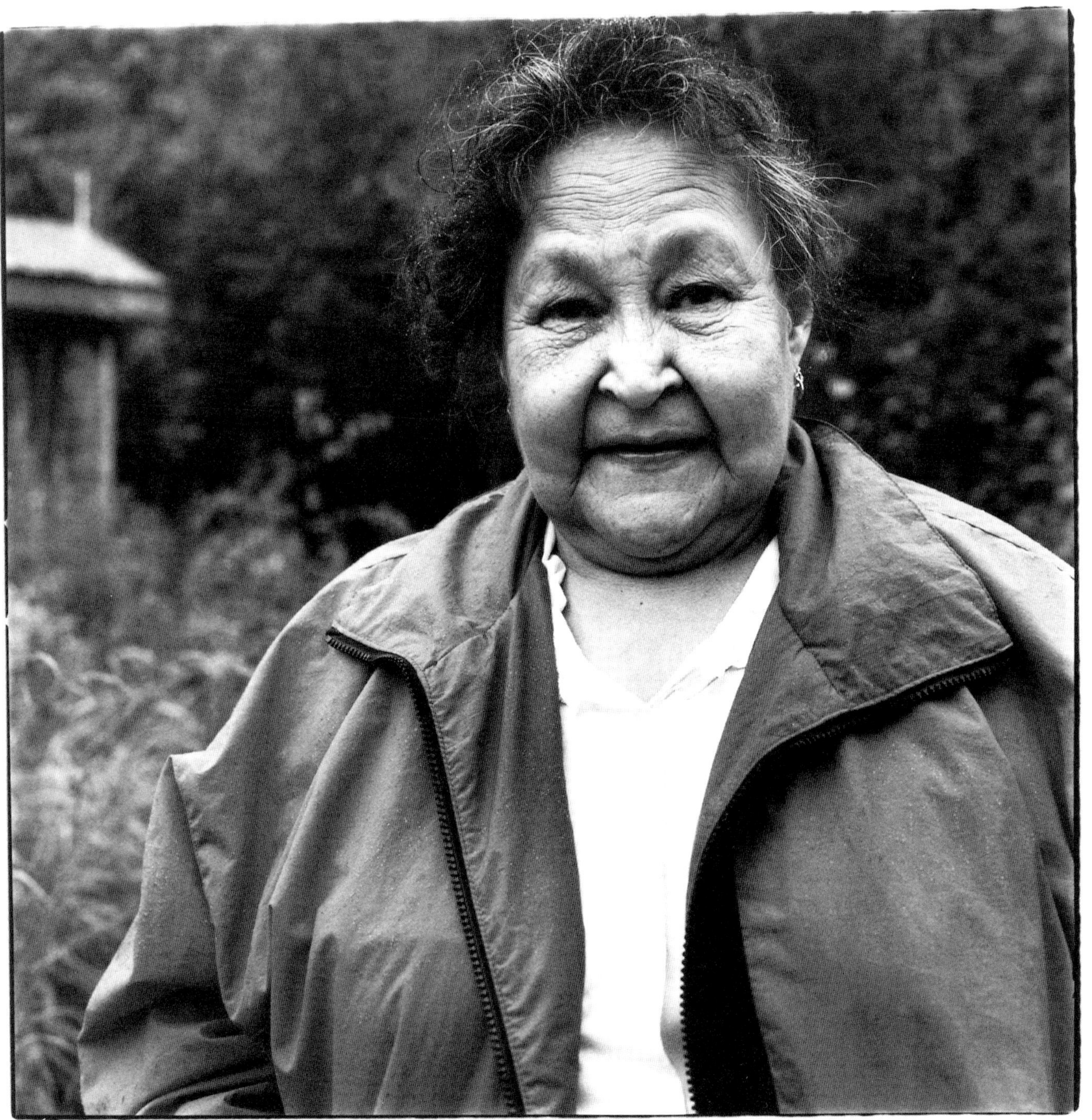

September 6

Verla Faye Aloyius
Holy Cross, AK

Lillian Walker's granddaughter, Verla Faye, was born in 1973 and grew up in Holy Cross. Three weeks before graduating from high school, she had an experience that changed her life.

The accident

I got hit by a motorcycle three weeks before graduation. A week before my 18th birthday. Me and my friend were out walking. Everyone walks down to the airport in the springtime. We heard a motorcycle, but we thought it was on the hillside. It was dark, he was drunk. He didn't have no headlight. He hit me. It happened on a Saturday night and I was knocked out until the next Wednesday. It changed me a lot. Before that, I was just like everybody else around here. Growing up and drinking 'cause everybody does that. I started to do that too. After getting hit and everything, I stopped. I lost friends just because I wasn't drinking and running around like I used to. I was depressed for a long time after that.

Lonesome for Holy Cross

I worked in the canneries in Emmonak for two years. It's fun. I think I'm ready to go to Anchorage. To me right now, Holy Cross is going down. Everybody's leaving. No matter what, they always come back, though. I get lonesome for Holy Cross. I don't know why.

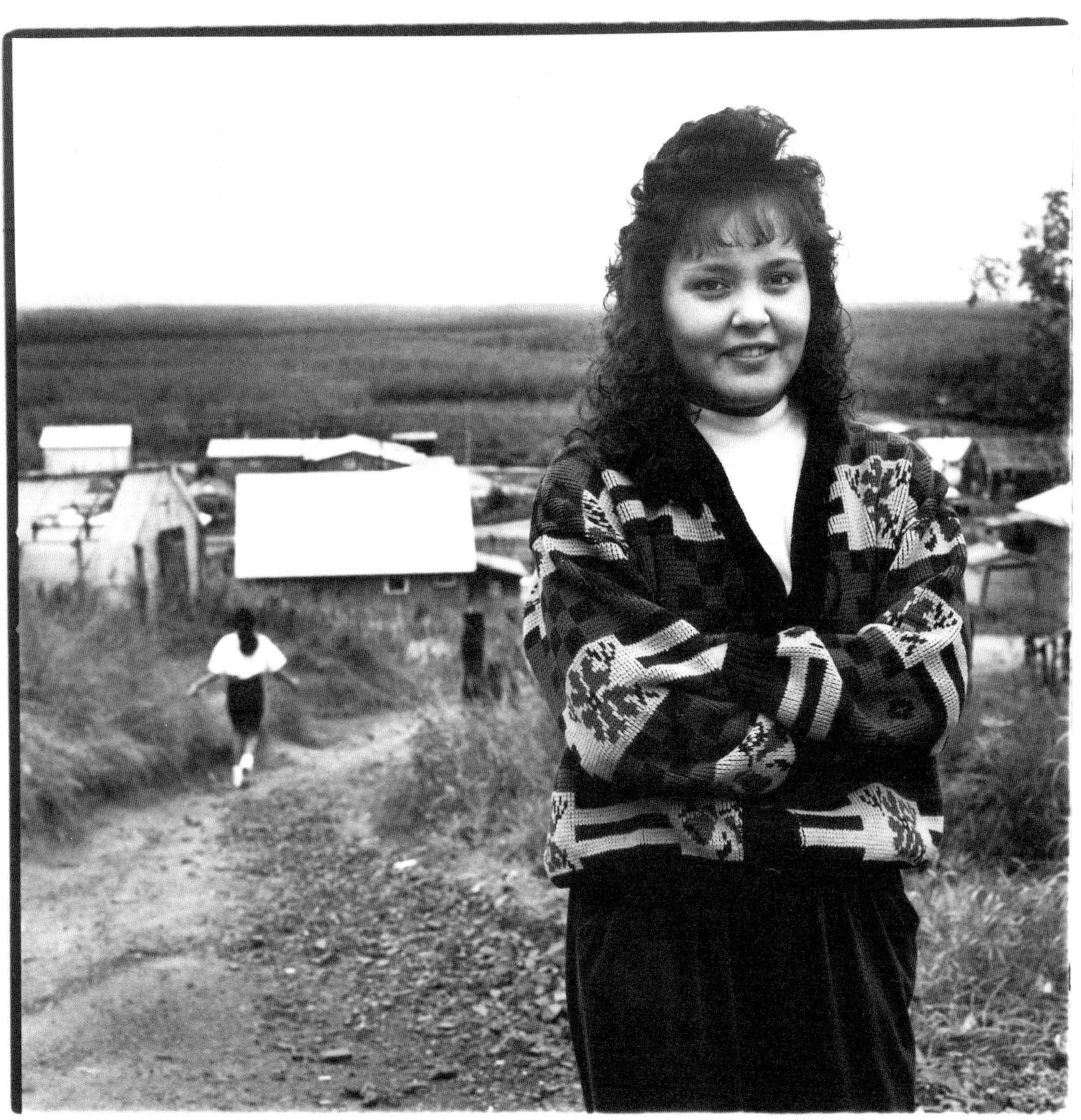

September 10

Sandra Kozevnikoff
Russian Mission, AK

Sandra was born in Russian Mission in 1947. She and her husband have five children. Sandra is presently the Yu'pic language teacher in the Russian Mission school.

Portages

I was born here. So was my father. I go to those old portages and I think of my forefathers. I think, "This trail is what my forefathers made and here I am jumping on it." And I kind of talk to my forefathers. I say, "I'm proud of you, grandparents, for making this trail for us." We still use a lot of those trails. If I go to New York or somewhere, I'll have no trails to thank my forefathers for. Even if I moved 20 miles downriver to Pitkas Point, I might not know where to go.

What her old ancestors say

We used to hunt for anything we wanted to eat when I was growing up. Moose anytime, bear, ducks, birds. Nobody wasted nothing of that stuff. Nothing was ever wasted. Even the bones. We put them under a tree or back into the lake where we got them from so their spirits can give us more food. People never got too much. There were no refrigerators and freezers and stuff. If we wanted meat, somebody went out and got moose or bear and just divided it up. The whole village would get it. And then the whole thing would be gone and they'd get another one.

Fish and Game really make us mad. They do all kinds of regulations. My old ancestors say, "Whatever you do, don't fight over a little piece of this and a little piece of that or the keeper of the earth will take it away from us." Sure enough, fish is declining in the river, some birds are almost all gone, reindeer herd they said has completely died. That's what we grew up with. That's our food. Moose and fish and birds. They're our food. They're the ones that make us strong and healthy.

Coke bottle

Everything speed up so fast. Too fast. It's like it puts everybody inside of a coke bottle and spins it around. We're whirling around in that bottle. The kids are worse off than me. They're more in that bottle. They're being Westernized more. They want to leave off their Yu'pic. I try to get them to learn their identity. They're really confused. Caught between two worlds.

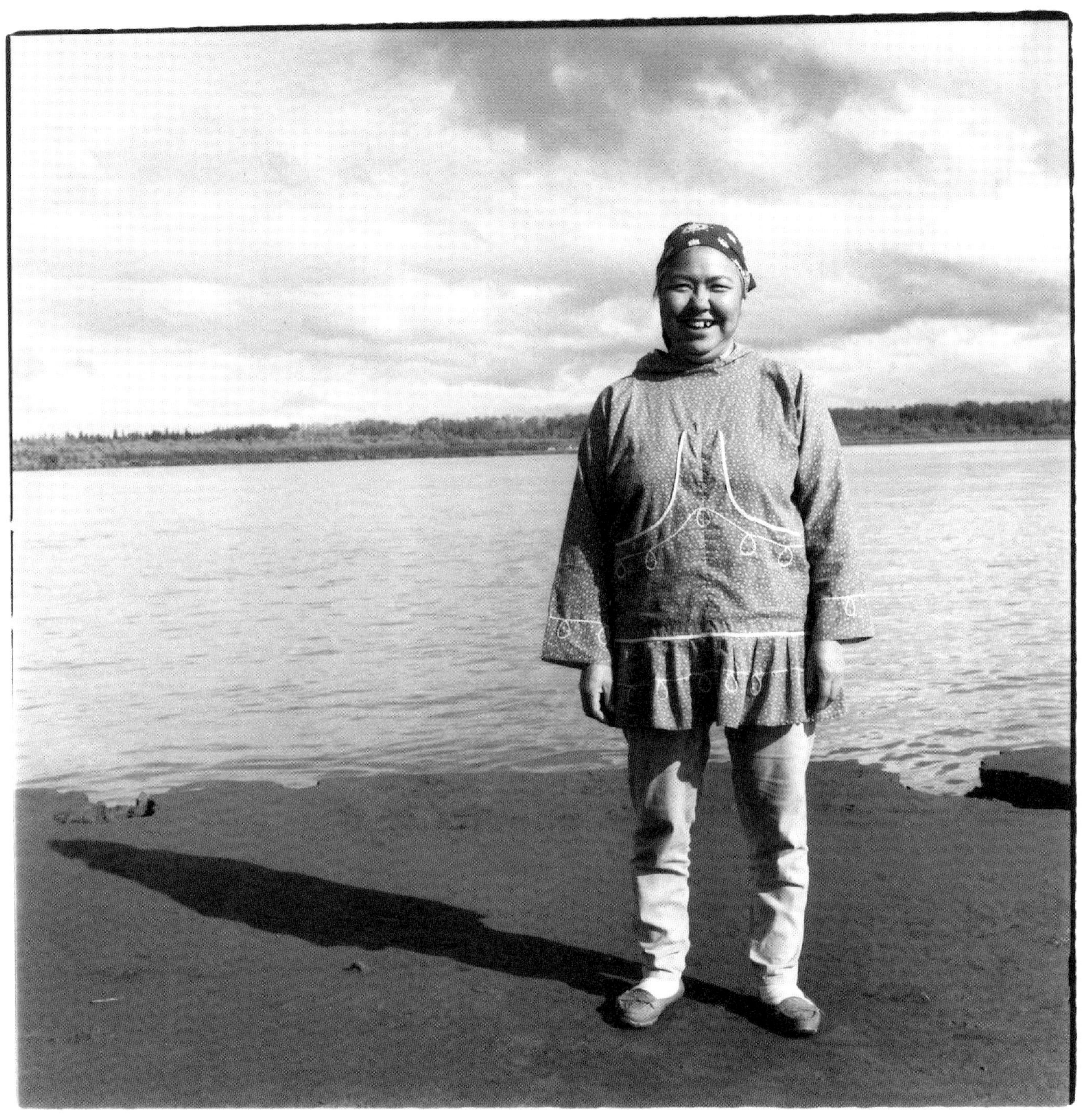

Pilot Station to Emmonak, Alaska

"My Heart" Milepost 1,795, Pitkas Point • *Proverbs*

Like ocean waves, the willows bend and flex in the howling wind as we try to leave Pilot Station for the third time. Then, as before, the wind drives us back to town.

"The one thing you don't plan for will go wrong," my father had replied four months earlier, after I said, "You know, we're so well prepared, I can't imagine one thing that could possibly go wrong." Fond of the compact wisdom of proverbs, my father's speech is peppered with Dutch sayings like, "*Vee vat spartr, vee vat hafe*" (He who saves is he who has), and the puzzling, *"Lekker is marr een finger lang"* (Tasty is only a finger long).

The fourth and last time we leave Pilot Station, the wind stops us, as before, a few miles from town. Some natives in Pilot Station confirm the weather report—the winds are here to stay. What to do? Two conflicting instincts battle within me. A conquering, white male attitude urges me to sprint to the end at any cost, while the advice that would come from a scowling, squinty-eyed, native fisherman urges me to respect the river enough to leave it. Can Kathleen make it? Can *I* make it? Watching muddy chunks of the bank break off and fall in the river under the pounding by restless waves, I realize how tired I am. This scares me more than anything else. Am I too tired to make the right decision?

Our celebratory champagne is too sweet and without substance—we don't finish the bottle. In Pilot Station the next day, I sell *My Heart* to a high school teacher, then we drive to the airport where a Jesuit priest flies us to the next village in his plane.

The next morning, we are walking through St. Marys' pleasantly unkempt graveyard when Kathleen points down to the river and says, "Monique—look!"

My heart stops when I see it. The surface of the river is completely smooth. That's when I notice the yellow leaves on a nearby tree are motionless. The wind has stopped.

"You know, I don't think it really matters how we finish the river—the most important part of this journey is the people and their stories," Kathleen says, tossing a rock into the water.

Then, as now, I know she is right, but part of me still wishes for the ultimate Hollywood ending—the two of us heroically defying the elements after three hellish days on the Yukon River delta, the wind dies as we paddle into a golden sunset . . .

Walking back to town, I wonder if my father knows of a proverb that could encapsulate all the joy, sadness, relief, pain, and pride I feel at stopping 150 miles short of finishing a 2,000 mile canoe trip, and after interviewing and photographing 85 people in less than 100 days.

All I can think of is, *"C'est la vie!"*

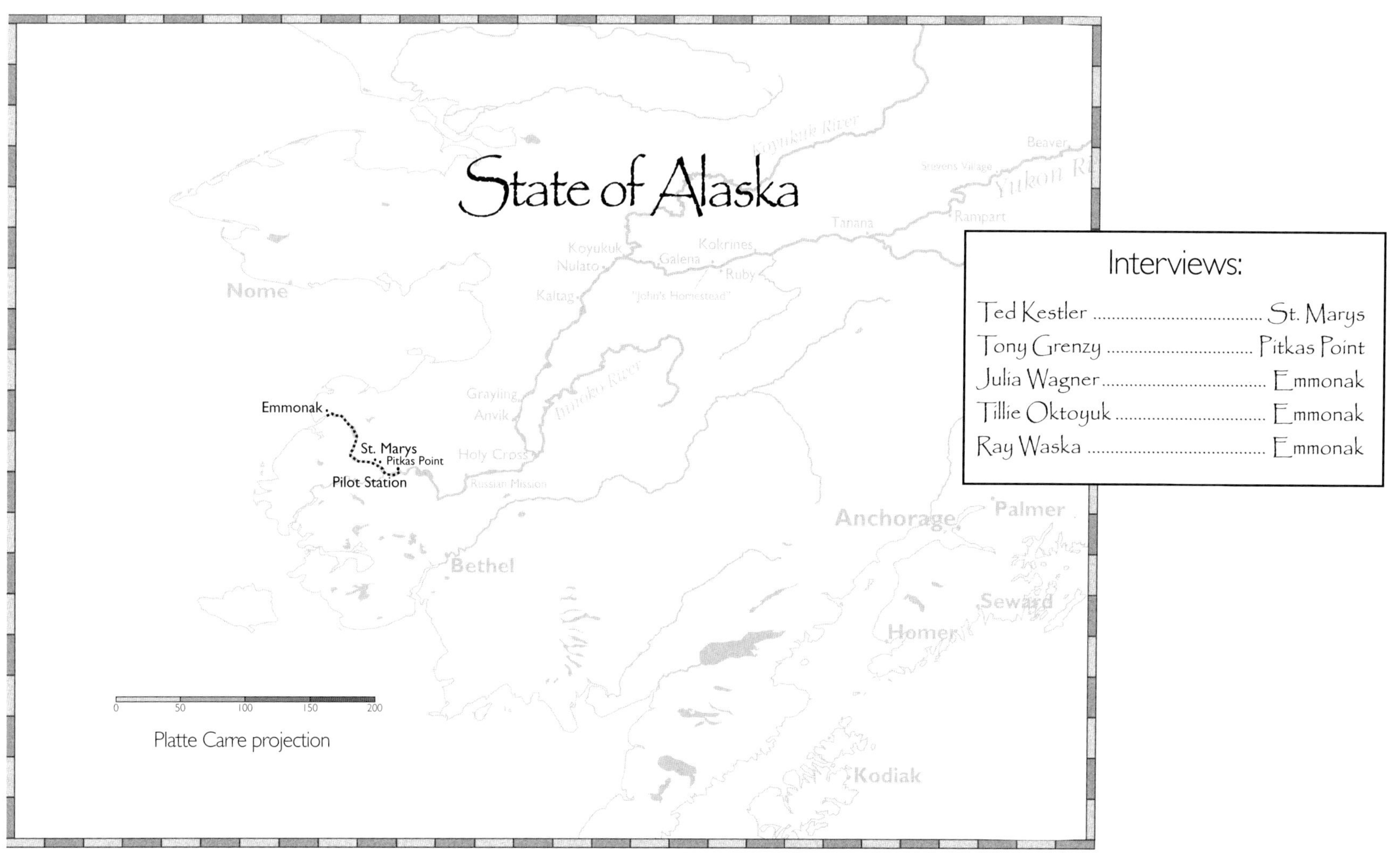
State of Alaska
Emmonak
St. Marys
Pitkas Point
Pilot Station
Nome
Koyukuk
Nulato
Kaltag
Galena
Kokrines
Ruby
"John's Homestead"
Tanana
Rampart
Beaver
Stevens Village
Yukon River
Koyukuk River
Innoko River
Grayling
Anvik
Holy Cross
Russian Mission
Bethel
Anchorage
Palmer
Seward
Homer
Kodiak
0 50 100 150 200
Platte Carre projection
Interviews:
Ted Kestler .... St. Marys
Tony Grenzy .... Pitkas Point
Julia Wagner .... Emmonak
Tillie Oktoyuk .... Emmonak
Ray Waska .... Emmonak

September 22

Ted Kestler
St. Marys, AK

Ted was born in 1943 in Tacoma, Washington. He attended college in Spokane, Berkeley, and Maine, earning degrees in chemistry, philosophy, and theology. Ted entered the Jesuit order in 1964. Before becoming ordained, Jesuit priests must do something they've never done before. Ted decided to go to Alaska. He now is the Jesuit Superior at the St. Marys Mission.

Burying young people

The people here have incredible gifts. I don't think I've ever met people as generous. Willing to share. A sense of hospitality. Of knowing suffering and weakness. I'd never been around a culture that was basically alcoholic.

There's a dry law in force right now in St. Marys, but there is an option to open up a liquor store whenever they want it. There is no question in my mind that it will mean burying 13 to 15 young people a year. But, if the people reflectively and honestly say we need to get this out in the open, and prohibition is not the way, then I have to respect that, even though I know it's going to mean a lot of pain and suffering. Of all the funerals I did in the Kaltag area, I had no funeral for anybody under 35 that wasn't alcohol related. I think, in four years, I counted 22 funerals, three of which were non-alcohol related.

As long as drinking is something that's happening to them rather than something that they're doing to themselves, I don't think it's going to end.

Christian symbols

My basic philosophic traditions center around Christian symbols. For me, the symbol of the cross is that there is hope in hopelessness. If people continue with the struggle, then there will be life, but I have to admit that that is a faith position. I don't have any proof of that.

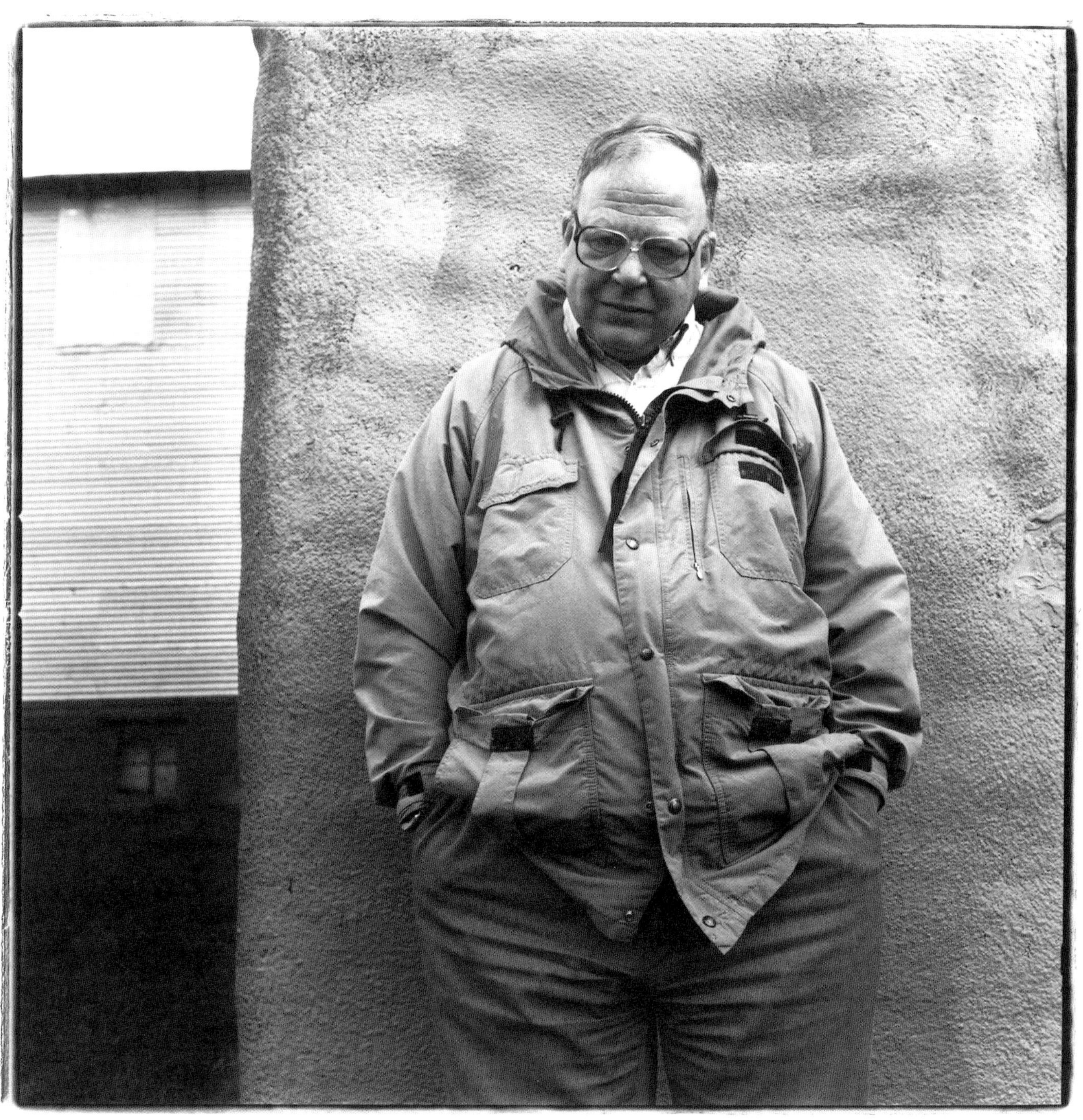

September 22

Tony Grenzy
Pitkas Point, AK

Tony was born in 1941 and grew up in Niagara Falls, New York. After finishing high school, he joined a seminary, spending several years there. After leaving, he taught at a girls' reformatory and later became the principal. In 1989, Tony saw a newspaper announcement for teaching jobs in Alaska. He applied and was hired as the school principal in Pitkas Point. Tony has been in Alaska for four years.

Virginia's house

I really feel like it's family here. I went up to Virginia's house tonight and I just dropped in. Everybody greeted me. That made me feel really good. She gave me my food first. I was laughing at myself because I was eating with my hands. They're passing a rag to wipe their hands on. I was joking, pretending to wipe my hands on my beard. I'm eating strips of fish which three years ago I wouldn't have gotten near. Whale blubber and stuff. It's part of me now. My whole way of eating has changed.

Expressing sorrow

Sometimes it's so depressing out here because of the drinking. I go to school on a Monday morning and I've got kids that are sleeping on the floors and on the desks. They'll come up to you and say they're scared to go home because their parents tried to strangle them because they were drunk. You just want to go up there and kill the parents. But then you stop and think. They're not working, they have no food, they're depressed. Drinking is their only way of getting it out. They're not a people that express themselves or their sorrow. When they've been drinking, they do.

Being the mother, the father, the grandfather, the aunt, the uncle

They come to school, they haven't washed. They're unkempt. So we have the kids bring clean clothes to school—the little kids. We bathe them at school, we make them brush their teeth, we give them shampoo, we dry their hair. Everything is given to them. You wash their dirty clothes, you take them to the doctor. You're the mother, the father, the grandfather, the aunt, the uncle.

You have to flow with it. You can't be a missionary. These people have lived here for thousands of years. They're probably going to be here thousands of years after I'm gone. I'm not going to change it. I'm here to try to make it better.

Fading away

I really think that the state of Alaska wishes we were all dead out here. There's no reason why this village should not have running water. Or a doctor to come out once a month. They shouldn't have tuberculosis in this day and age . . . meningitis . . . hepatitis . . . It's really sad. They should have somebody in these villages for drug counseling, for alcohol counseling, for child abuse. I really think that the state of Alaska really doesn't care about them out here. If they all got drunk and faded away, it would be just wonderful.

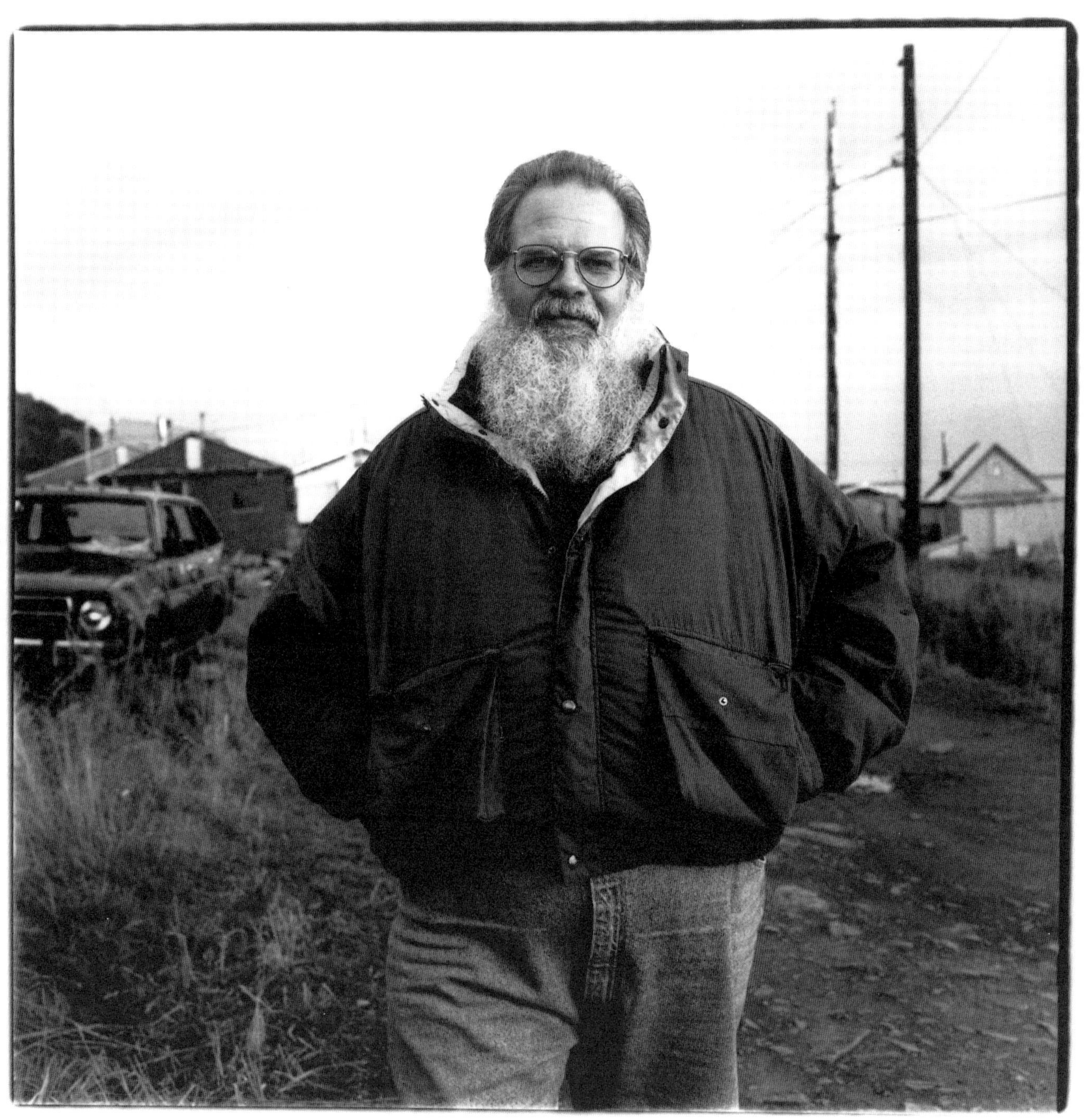

September 27

Julia Wagner
Emmonak, AK

Julia was born in Emmonak in 1952. After attending high school in Oklahoma and Anchorage, she returned to Emmonak. Julia is married and has two daughters, and is deeply involved in Eskimo dancing.

Perfect Pennsylvania

When I went to school in Oklahoma, the other students used to ask me, "Do you guys really live in igloos?"

I used to lie—I say I have 2 to 3 story igloo and we have rabbit skins for blanket and pillows. Sealskin for the bottom. Really ice cold swimming pool. Little things we say, they used to believe us.

One time we went to Pennsylvania. It was so perfect. Perfect everything, you know, organized. The grass was mowed and the house was spick-and-span and we eat so nice, you know. Everything so organized. Everything so nice.

Junk

All the junk from way upriver comes down here to the coast. It goes all the way to where we hunt. The junk at the bottom is piling up. There's more junk now than we ever had before. We didn't have junk long time ago. Not like we do now.

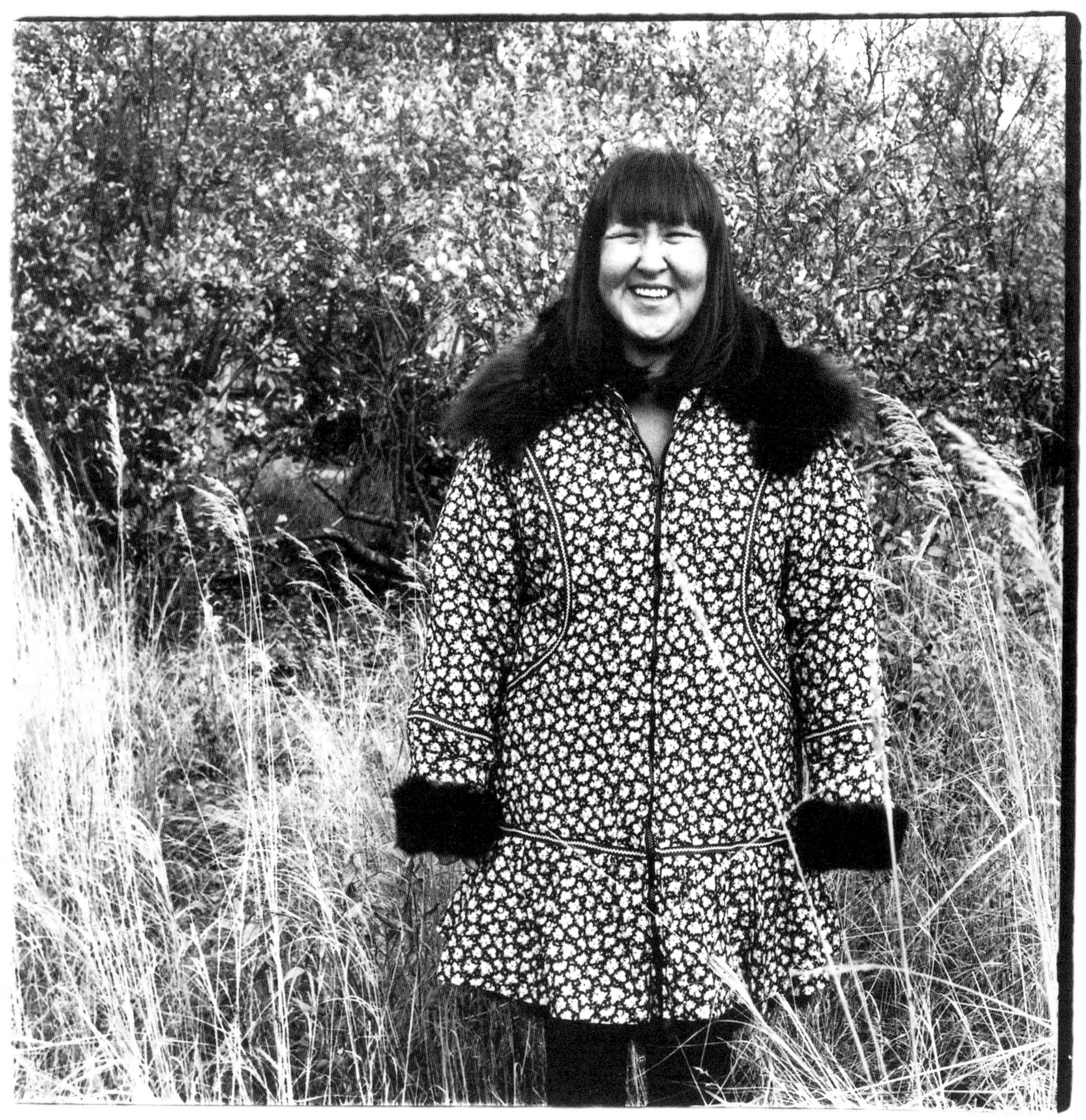

September 27

Tillie Oktoyuk
Emmonak, AK

One of ten children, Tillie was born in 1952 in Alakanuk, Alaska. Besides attending school in her village, she went to the Bureau of Indian Affairs school in Wrangle and completed two years of college in Montana. Tillie has worked as the secretary of the Emmonak school, in a fish packing plant, and for the City of Emmonak. She is presently an accountant at the Fish Marketing Co-op, the only native-owned fishery in the Yukon delta. Tillie and her husband were married in 1973, and have three children.

The change

People used to live more off the land. Right now it's more store bought. It's more store bought than off the land. We've changed from a subsistence life to a more cash economy. And fast. And we have all the problems that go with change. A lot of people are trying to become accustomed to the white way of living. I still have to go out and gather food. I was brought up that way—to eat off the land.

Smiling in Chicago

I appreciate living in the village now. We don't have muggings or whatever else is out there. It's a scary world out there. It is. People are very unfriendly.

I remember walking in Chicago and my girlfriend saying, "Hang on to your purse. Don't smile at anybody."

Here I am from a small town where everybody is friendly and they'll stop and give you a hand if you need help. Out there, you could be on the street dying and they'd pass you.

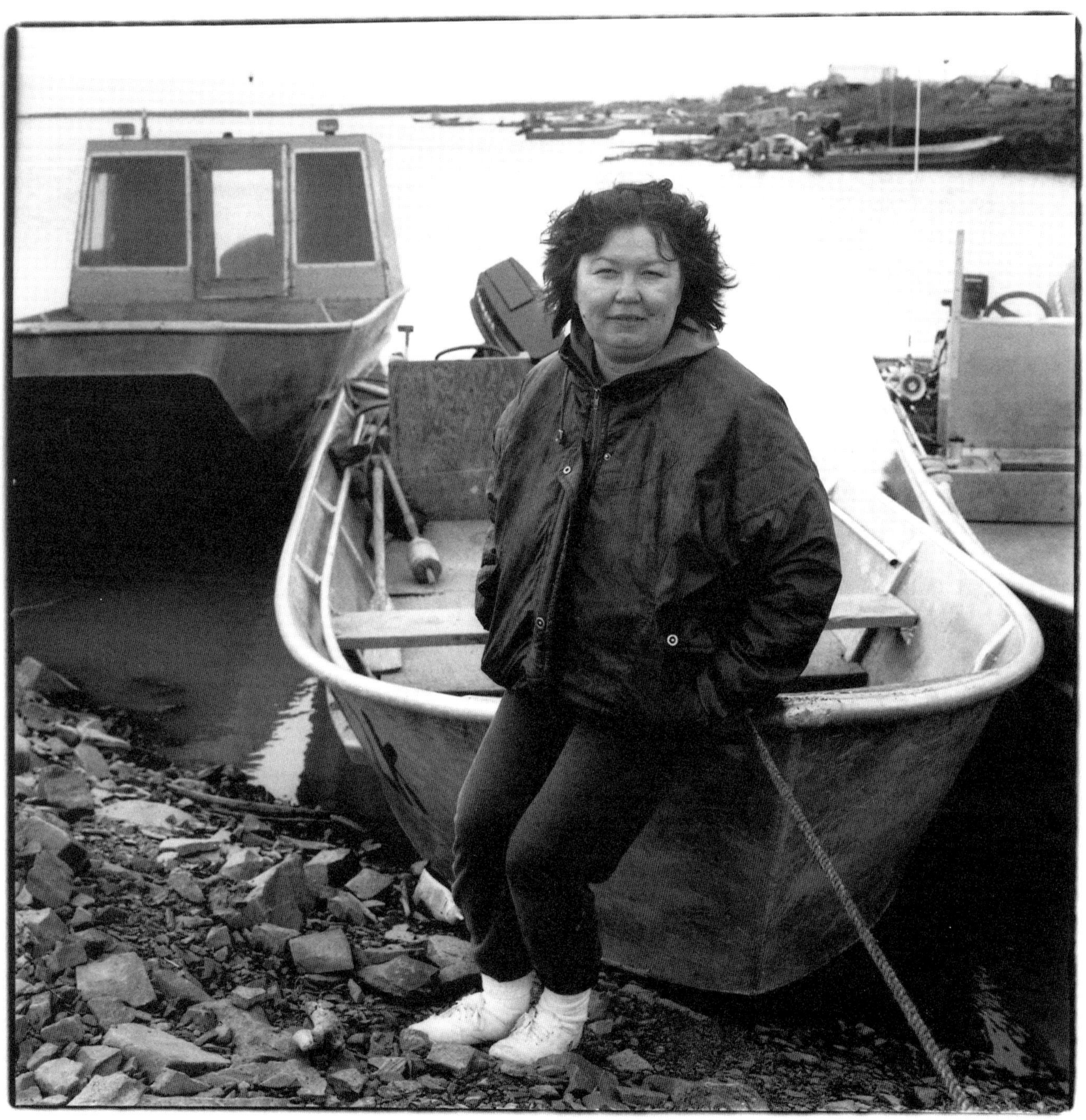

September 27

Ray Waska
Emmonak, AK

Ray was born in 1941 and raised in Emmonak. His mother died when he was very young and all of his 11 siblings died of spinal meningitis. A self-professed jack of all trades, he has been everything from a church deacon to a marriage counselor. Ray and his wife Laurie were married in 1965, and they have nine children. Ray presently works in the hardware department of one of the local stores.

Think right

Young people, if they think right, should follow the old ways and the white man's ways. Combine both together. The white part is to follow the rules, like city ordinances, stay out of trouble, and work. The old ways—respect each other, but first of all, respect themselves. First, they need to explore themselves. Our mistake was not talking to them in Yu'pic, but now they're older and they're trying. It's up to them. A guy who's going to follow the native culture, he's going to have to speak Yu'pic.

Read, read, read

I earned my education through reading. I had a teacher when I was going to boarding school. He said read books—read, read, read. Lot of people around here think I'm a high school graduate, but I'm not. I do a lot of reading. I still read—western books, Louis L'Amour. I think I have all of his novels. Reading Louis L'Amour books, it's just like studying early pioneer history in the lower states. He'd study the place and what was happening, and write a book.

Shamans keeping to themselves

That's what we need around here. We need shamans. There were shamans in the old days, but the religious people thought it was wrong. They thought it was evil spirits, but now they find out it wasn't so, and they started apologizing. Shamans—one was the weather predictor, one was the healer, one was a counselor. There could be some here, but I don't know. It's too bad they're keeping to themselves. There might be some around, it's hard to tell.

The river

The river is my highway. My freezer. My warehouse. My food storage. If I'm not lazy, I'll get food from the river. If I'm lazy, I wouldn't get it. River, I tell you, is a K-Mart. It's a K-Mart. It could be your worst enemy, too. Your worst enemy in the world.

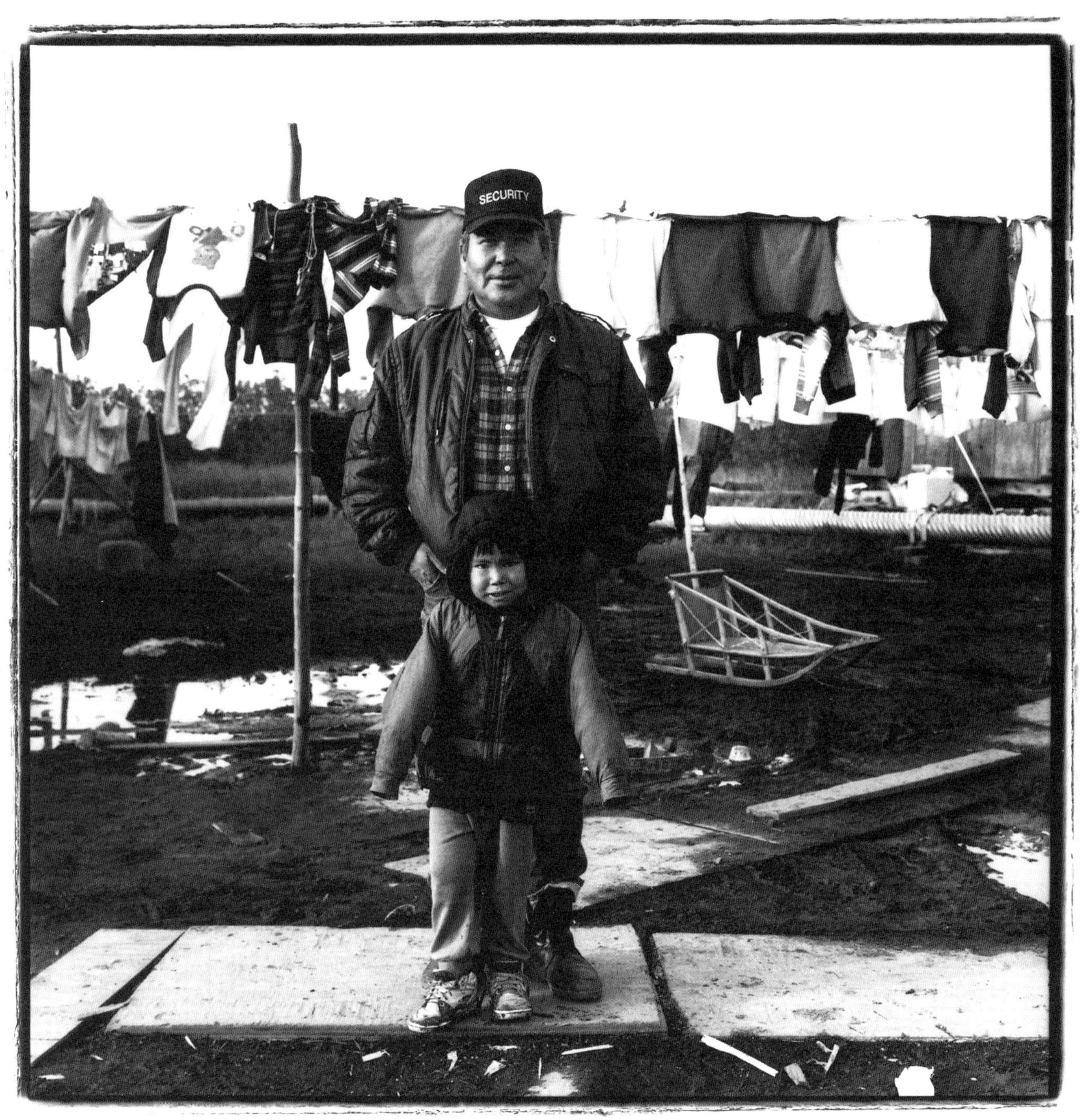
SECURITY

"My Heart" Milepost 1,995, Emmonak • *From the Yukon to the Hudson*

Flying to the last three villages, our remaining week is a blur of hastily conducted interviews and taking portraits of people lashed by the icy fall wind. It is not until we clink coffee cups in an Emmonak diner—the trip suddenly and unremarkably over—that I realize how different this journey would have been had it not been made by canoe.

The difference between flying and paddling is like the difference between seeing Niagara Falls from an air-conditioned bus and going over it in a barrel. By paddling, we became part of the river, giving us kinship and closeness to the people we were interviewing. By flying, Kathleen and I became two city girls with an intrusive microphone and some flashy camera gear. We became "outsiders" again.

Canoeing between villages gave us the time to talk about the people we were interviewing, whether the baby moose we'd seen swimming in the river had made it safely across, how far it was to the next village, and what we were going to eat for supper that night. The roar of the airplane made conversation impossible, so we looked out the window instead.

The river is a humbling sight from the air—a dark trench cutting through the land as far as the eye can see. Would we have done this trip if we'd known how big the river really was? And the waves! Instead of fierce and random chaos, however, the waves are tidy rows of lacy crescents.

"Easy as pie," I say to Kathleen in Emmonak's coffee shop. "Those waves looked as easy as pie from the air. I can't believe it!"

Breaking her sightless gaze from the menu posted over the large, grease-spattered grill, Kathleen answers, "I still can't believe the trip is really over."

Following her into the sharp fall sunshine a few minutes later and turning automatically to look at the river, I know exactly what she means. I also think how beginnings are better than endings, and that middles are better than both.

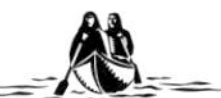

The thick-necked taxi driver stabs a dirty thumb towards the Statue of Liberty and says, "There she is girls," briefly interrupting his rambling monologue about scoundrel taxi drivers. He is still talking half an hour later when he drops us off in the East Village, in front of Kathleen's cousin's apartment. Bruce, a stockbroker, is still at work, so Kathleen gets the key from the hardware store downstairs as instructed.

The muddy canoe packs—so functional and sturdy on the river—look completely out of place in Bruce's nice Manhattan apartment. Suddenly, I desperately need fresh air. It is too much too soon—from canoe to yellow cab, from fishermen to stockbrokers, and from a tiny Eskimo village to swarming metropolis.

"Hey, let's go out and eat somewhere," I say, heading for the door.

Jazz, warm and honey-like, is playing when we enter the restaurant. The waiter, wearing leather pants and a crisp white shirt, coldly says, "For two?" and leads us to our seats. I pick at my black squid pasta while Kathleen stares sleepily at a mountain of Caesar salad. We don't stay long. Rushing into haute cuisine after months of Yukon River salmon is almost as jarring as arriving at the Manhattan apartment.

Back at Bruce's place, Kathleen falls asleep on the white, velvety sofa, a shaft of sunlight slicing across her heavily muscled arm. Sinking in a deep chair by the window, I am soon lulled to sleep by the incessant melody of taxi horns honking in the street below.